# Elements of Civil Government

## by Alexander L. Peterman

I0450540

DEDICATION.

To the thousands of devoted Teachers in every part of the land, who are training the boys and girls of to-day to a true conception of American citizenship, and to a deeper love for our whole country, this little book is dedicated by a Brother in the work.

# PREFACE.

This text-book begins "at home." The starting-point is the family, the first form of government with which the child comes in contact. As his acquaintance with rightful authority increases, the school, the civil district, the township, the county, the State, and the United States are taken up in their order.

The book is especially intended for use in the public schools. The plan is the simplest yet devised, and is, therefore, well adapted to public school purposes. It has been used by the author for many years, in public schools, normal schools, and teachers' institutes. It carefully and logically follows the much praised and much neglected synthetic method. All students of the science of teaching agree that beginners in the study of government should commence with the known, and gradually proceed to the unknown. Yet it is believed this is the first textbook that closely follows this method of treating the subject.

The constant aim has been to present the subject in a simple and attractive way, in accordance with sound principles of teaching--that children may grow into such a knowledge of their government that the welfare of the country may "come home to the business and bosoms" of the people.

The recent increase of interest among the people upon the subject of government is a hopeful sign. It will lead to a better knowledge of our political institutions, and hence give us better citizens. Good citizenship is impossible unless the people understand the government under which they live.

It is certainly strange that every State in the Union maintains a system of public schools for the purpose of training citizens, and that the course of study in so many States omits civil government, the science of citizenship.

The author's special thanks are due Hon. Joseph Desha Pickett, Ph.D., Superintendent of Public Instruction of Kentucky, for the suggestion which led to the preparation of the work and for excellent thoughts upon the plan. The author also desires to confess his obligation to President James K. Patterson, Ph.D., and Professor R. N. Roark, A.M., of the Kentucky State College, Lexington, for valuable suggestions as to the method of treatment and the scope of the book.

The author has derived much assistance from the many admirable works upon the same subject, now before the country. But he has not hesitated to adopt a treatment different from theirs when it has been deemed advisable. He submits his work to a discriminating public, with the hope that he has not labored in vain in a field in which so many have wrought.

ALEX. L. PETERMAN.

## A FEW WORDS TO TEACHERS.

1. PURPOSE OF THE STUDY.--Every school should teach, and every child should study, the principles of our government, in order:

1. That by knowing his country better he may learn to love it more. The first duty of the school is to teach its pupils to love "God, home, and native land."

2. That the child may learn that there is such a thing as just authority; that obedience to it is right and manly; that we must learn to govern by first learning to obey.

3. That he may know his rights as a citizen, and, "knowing, dare maintain;" that he may also know his duties as a citizen, and, knowing, may perform them intelligently and honestly.

4. That he may understand the sacredness of the right of suffrage, and aid in securing honest elections and honest discharge of official duties.

5. That he may better understand the history of his country, for the history of the United States is largely the history of our political institutions.

2. ORAL INSTRUCTION.--There is no child in your school too young to learn something of geography, of history, and of civil government.

These three subjects are so closely related that it is easier and better to teach them together. All pupils not prepared for the text-book should, at least on alternate days, be instructed by the teacher in a series of familiar talks, beginning with "The Family," and proceeding slowly to "The School," "The

Civil District or Township," "The County," "The State," and "The United States." In this system of oral instruction, which is the best possible preparation for the formal study of civil government, the plan and outlines of this book may be used by the teacher with both profit and pleasure.

3. PROPER AGE FOR STUDY OF THE TEXT-BOOK.--The plan and the style of this book are so simple that the subject will be readily understood by pupils reading in the "Fourth Reader." Even in our ungraded country schools the average pupil of twelve years is well prepared to begin the study of the text-book in civil government. It is a serious mistake to postpone this much neglected subject until a later age. Let it be introduced early, that the child's knowledge of his government may "grow with his growth, and strengthen with his strength."

4. TWO PARTS.--It will be observed that the book is divided into two parts: the former treating the subject concretely, the latter treating it abstractly.

Beginners should deal with things, not theories; hence, the abstract treatment of civil government is deferred until the pupil's mind is able to grasp it.

For the same reason, definitions in the first part of the book are few and simple, the design of the author being to illustrate rather than to define; to lead the child to see, rather than to burden his mind with fine-spun statements that serve only to confuse. In an elaborate work for advanced students the method of treatment would, of course, be quite different.

5. TOPICAL METHOD.--The subject of each paragraph is printed in bold-faced type, thus specially adapting the book to the topical method of recitation. This feature also serves as a guide to the pupil in the preparation of his lesson.

6. SUGGESTIVE QUESTIONS.--In deference to the best professional thought, the author has omitted all questions upon the text, knowing that every live teacher prefers to frame his own questions. The space usually allotted to questions upon the text is devoted to suggestive questions, intended to lead the pupil to think and to investigate for himself.

The author sincerely hopes that the teacher will not permit the pupil to memorize the language of the book, but encourage him to express the thought in his own words.

# CONTENTS.

THE COUNTY.

Introductory; Purposes; Formation; Area; County Seat; Government; Corporate Power; Departments; Officers; Legislative Department; County Commissioners, or Board of Supervisors; Executive Department; County, Attorney, or Prosecuting Attorney; County Superintendent of Schools; Sheriff; Treasurer; Auditor; County Clerk, or Common Pleas Clerk; Recorder, or Register; Surveyor; Coroner; Other Officers; Judicial Department; County Judge, or Probate Judge; Suggestive Questions

CHAPTER VI.

MUNICIPAL CORPORATIONS--VILLAGES, BOROUGHS, AND CITIES.

The Village or Borough; Incorporation; Government; Officers; Duties; The City; Incorporation; Wards; City Institutions; Finances; Citizens; Rights and Duties; Government; Officers; Duties; Commission Plan of City Government; Recall; Suggestive Questions

CHAPTER VII.

THE STATE

Introductory; Definition; Formation of Original States; Admission of New States; Purposes; Functions; Institutions; Citizens; Rights; Duties; Constitution; Formation and Adoption; Purposes; Value; Contents; Bill of Rights; Suggestive Questions

CHAPTER VIII.

THE STATE--(Continued).

Government Departments; Legislative Department; Qualifications; Privileges; Power; Sessions; Functions; Forbidden Powers; The Senate; House of Representatives; Direct Legislation; Suggestive Questions

CHAPTER IX.

# ELEMENTS OF CIVIL GOVERNMENT

## PART I.

## CHAPTER I.

## THE FAMILY.

INTRODUCTORY.[1]--People living in the United States owe respect and obedience to not less than four different governments; that is, to four forms of organized authority. They have duties, as citizens of a township or civil district, as citizens of a county, as citizens of some one of the States, and as citizens of the United States. All persons are, or have been, members of a family; some also live under a village or city government; and most children are subject to the government, of some school. Many people in this country live under six governments--namely, the family, the township or civil district, the village or city, the county, the State, and the United States; while children who live in villages or cities, and attend school, are subject to seven different governments. These organizations are so closely related that the duties of the people as citizens of one do not conflict with their duties as citizens of the others. The better citizen a person is of one of these governments the better citizen he is of all governments under which he lives.

DEFINITION.--Each of us is a member of some family. We were born into the family circle, and our parents first taught us to obey. By insisting upon obedience, parents govern their children, and thus keep them from evil and from danger. The family, then, is a form of government, established for the good of the children themselves, and the first government that each of us must obey.

PURPOSES.--The family exists for the rearing and training of children, and for the happiness and prosperity of parents. All children need the comforts and restraints of home life. They are growing up to be citizens and rulers of the country, and should learn to rule by first learning to obey. The lessons of home prepare them for life and for citizenship.

MEMBERS.

The members of the family are the father, the mother, and the children; and the family government exists for all, especially for the children, that they may be protected, guided, and taught to become useful men and women. The welfare of each and of all depends upon the family government, upon the care of the parents and the obedience of the children.

RIGHTS.--The members have certain rights; that is, certain just claims upon the family. Each has a right to all the care and protection that the family can give: a right to be kindly treated; a right to be spoken to in a polite manner; a right to food, clothing, shelter, and an opportunity to acquire an education; a right to the advice and warning of the older members; a right to the respect of all.

DUTIES.--As each of the members has his rights, each also has his duties; for where a right exists, a duty always exists with it. It is the duty of each to treat the others kindly; to teach them what is right and what is wrong; to aid them in their work; to comfort them in their sorrows; and to rejoice with them in their gladness. It is the duty of the children to love their parents; to obey them in all things; to respect older persons; and to abstain from bad habits and bad language.

OFFICERS.

The officers of the family government are the father and the mother. They were made officers when they were married, so that the rulers of the family are also members of the family. The office of a parent is a holy office, and requires wisdom for the proper discharge of its duties.

POWERS.--The parents have power to make rules, to decide when these have been broken, and to insist that they shall be obeyed. They make the law of the family, enforce the law, and explain the law. They have supreme control over their children in all the usual affairs of life, until the children arrive at the legal age--twenty-one years.

DUTIES, RESPONSIBILITY.--Parents should be firm and just in their rulings; they should study the welfare of their children, and use every effort to train them to lives of usefulness and honor. It is the duty of parents to provide their children with food, clothing, shelter, and the means of acquiring an education. There is no other responsibility so great as the responsibility of fathers and mothers. They are responsible for themselves, and the law makes them partly responsible for the conduct of their children. Therefore, one of the highest duties of a parent to his children is to exact obedience in all right things, in order that the children may be trained to true manhood and womanhood.

[1]To the teacher--Do not assign to the average class more than two or three pages of the text as a lesson. Make haste slowly. When each chapter is completed let it be reviewed at once, while the pupil's interest is fresh.

See that the "Suggestive Questions" at the end of the chapter are not neglected. If necessary, devote special lessons to their consideration. Assign the "questions" to the members of the class, to be answered on the following day, giving not more than two "questions" to any pupil.

SUGGESTIVE QUESTIONS.

1. Name some of the restraints of home life.

2. Why does the welfare of all depend upon the family government?

3. Why do rights and duties always exist together?

4. Name some bad habits.

5. Why should children abstain from bad habits?

6. What is true manhood?

7. Are disobedient children apt to make good citizens?

8. Should a father permit his bad habits to be adopted by his children?

CHAPTER II.

THE SCHOOL.

INTRODUCTORY.--When children reach the age of six or seven years, they enter the public school and become subject to its rules. We are born under government, and we are educated under it. We are under it at home, in school, and in after life. Law and order are everywhere necessary to the peace, safety, liberty, and' happiness of the people. True liberty and true enlightenment can not exist unless regulated by law.

DEFINITION AND PURPOSES.--A school district or sub-district is a certain portion of the town or county laid off and set apart for the purpose of establishing and maintaining a public school. It exists for educational reasons only, and is the unit of educational work. The public schools are supported by funds raised partly by the State, and partly by the county or the township. They are frequently called common schools or free schools. It is the duty of the State to provide all children with the means of acquiring a plain English education, and the State discharges this duty by dividing the county into districts of such size that a school-house and a public school arc within reach of every child.

FORMATION.--The limits of the school district are usually fixed by the chief school officer of the county, by the town, by the school board, or by the people living in the neighborhood. In most of the States districts vary greatly in size and shape; but in some of the States they have a regular form, each being about two miles square.

FUNCTIONS.--The functions, or work, of the school are solely educational. The State supports a system of public schools in order that the masses of the people may be educated. The country needs good citizens: to be good citizens the people must be intelligent, and to be intelligent they must attend School.

MEMBERS.

The members of the school district are the people living in it. All are interested, one way or another, in the success of the school. In most States the legal voters elect the school board, or trustees, and in some States levy the district school taxes. Those who are neither voters nor within the school age are interested in the intelligence and good name of the community, and are therefore interested in the public school.

CHILDREN.--The children within the-school age are the members of the school, and they are the most important members of the school district. It is for their good that the school exists. The State has provided schools in order that its children may be educated, and thus become useful men and women and good citizens.

RIGHTS.--Children, as members of the school, have important rights and duties. It is the right, one of the highest rights, of every child to attend the full session of the public school. Whoever prevents him from exercising this right commits an offense against the child and against the State. The State taxes its citizens to maintain a system of schools for the benefit of every child, and so every child has a right to all the State has provided for him.

DUTIES.--As it is the right, it is also the duty of all children to attend the full session of the public school, or of some other equally good. They should be regular and punctual in their attendance; they should yield prompt and cheerful obedience to the school government, and try to avail themselves of all advantages that the school can give. As it is the duty of the State to offer a plain English education to every child, so it is the duty of all children to make the most of all means the State has provided for their education.

PARENTS, THEIR RIGHTS AND DUTIES.--All parents have the right to send their children to the public school, and it is also their duty to patronize the public school, or some other equally as good. Fathers and mothers who deprive their children of the opportunities of acquiring an education do them lasting injury. Parents should use every effort to give their children at least the best education that can be obtained in the public schools.

GOVERNMENT.

The school has rules to govern it, that the pupil may be guided, directed, and protected in the pursuit of knowledge. Schools can not work without order, and there can be no order without government. The members of the school desire that good order be maintained, for they know their success depends upon it; so that school, government, like all other good government, exists by the consent and for the good of the governed.

OFFICERS.--The school, like all other governments, has its officers. These are the school board, or trustees, and the teacher. They are responsible for the government and good conduct of the school. There are, in most governments, three kinds of officers, corresponding to the three departments of government--the legislative, the judicial, and the executive. The legislative department of the government makes the laws, the judicial department explains them, and the executive department executes them. School officers are mostly executive; that is, their chief duties are to enforce the laws made by the legislature for the government of the public schools. As they also make rules for the school, their duties are partly legislative.

APPOINTMENT, TERM OF OFFICE.--The district officers are usually elected by the legal voters of the school district; but in some States they are appointed by the county superintendent, or county school commissioner as he is often called. In most States the term of office is three years, but in some it is two years, and in others it is only one year. Trustees or directors usually receive no pay for their services.

DUTIES.--In most States it is the duty of the district officers to raise money by levying taxes for the erection of school-buildings, and to superintend their construction; to purchase furniture and apparatus; to care for the school property; to employ teachers and fix their salaries; to visit the school and direct its work; to take the school census; and to make reports to the higher school officers. In some States, as in Indiana, most of these duties belong to the office of township trustee.

THE TEACHER.--The teacher is usually employed by the directors or trustees, but in some States he is employed by the township trustee or by the county superintendent. He must first pass an examination before an examiner, or board of examiners, and obtain therefrom a certificate or license entitling him to teach in the public schools.

POWERS.--The teacher has the same power and right to govern the school that the parent has to govern the family. The law puts the teacher in the parent's place and expects him to perform the parent's office, subject to the action of the directors or trustees. It clothes him with all power necessary to govern the school, and then holds him responsible for its conduct, the directors having the right to dismiss him at any time for a failure to perform his duty.

DUTIES.--The teacher is one of our most important officers. The State has confided to him the trust of teaching, of showing boys and girls how to be useful men and women, of training them for citizenship. This is a great work to do. The State has clothed him with ample power for the purpose, and it is his duty to serve the State faithfully and well. The teacher should govern kindly and firmly. Every pupil in school, of whatever age or size, owes him cheerful and ready obedience. It is his duty, the duty for which he is paid, to insist upon this obedience; to govern the school; to teach the pupils to obey while they are children, in order that they may rule well when they become rulers; that is, when they become citizens.

SUGGESTIVE QUESTIONS.

1. Why are law and order necessary to the peace and happiness of the people?

2. Why are public schools sometimes called free schools or common schools?

3. About how many square miles are there in a school district in this county?

4. What is the official title, and what the name, of the chief school officer of this county?

5. Why does the State want its people educated?

6. Why should children be regular and punctual in their attendance?

7. What can parents do to aid their children to acquire an education?

8. What number of directors do you think would be best for the school district? Why?

9. Should directors receive compensation? How much?

10. Why should the teacher pass an examination?

11. Should he be examined every year?

12. Why does the law place the teacher in the parent's place?

13. Why are citizens said to be rulers?

QUESTION FOR DEBATE.

Resolved, That it is right for a man without children to pay school taxes.

CHAPTER III.

THE CIVIL DISTRICT.

INTRODUCTORY.--In our study, thus far, we have had to do with special forms of government as exercised in the family and in the school. These are, in a sense, peculiar to themselves. The rights of government as administered in the family, and the rights of the members of a family, as well as their duties to each other, are natural rights and duties; they do not depend upon society for their force. In fact, they are stronger and more binding in proportion as the bands of society are relaxed.

In the primitive state, before there was organized civil society, family government was supreme; and likewise, if a family should remove from within the limits of civil society and be entirely isolated, family government would again resume its power and binding force.

School government, while partaking of the nature of civil government, is still more closely allied to family government. In the natural state, and in the isolated household, the education of the child devolves upon the parents, and the parent delegates a part of his natural rights and duties to the teacher when he commits the education of his child to the common school. The teacher is said to stand in loco parentis (in the place of the parent), and from this direction, mainly, are his rights of government derived. The school, therefore, stands in an intermediate position between family government and civil government proper, partaking of some features of each, and forming a sort of stepping-stone for the child from the natural restraints of home to the more complex demands of civil society. The school district, also, while partaking of the nature of a civil institution, is in many respects to be regarded as a co-operative organization of the families of the neighborhood for the education of their children, and its government as a co-operative family government.

# THE CIVIL UNIT DEFINED.

In nearly every part of the United States there is a unit of civil society in which the people exercise many of the powers of government at first hand. This civil unit is variously named in the different States, and its first organization may have been for some minor purpose; but it has grown to be an important sphere of government in many States, and throughout the entire country it is the primary school of the citizen and the voter.

There are many different names by which this civil unit is known.

In the State of Mississippi it is called the Beat, and this name is no doubt derived from the original purpose of the organization, as the jurisdiction of a watchman or constable.

In Delaware it is called the Hundred, which is the old English subdivision of a county, supposed to contain one hundred families, or one hundred men able to bear arms in the public service.

In the New England States, in New York, and in Wisconsin it is called the Town, from the old Anglo-Saxon civil unit, which antedates the settlement of England by its Saxon invaders, and is probably older than the Christian era.

In Arkansas, Indiana, Iowa, Kansas, Michigan, Minnesota, Missouri, Montana, New Jersey, the Carolinas, Ohio, Pennsylvania, and parts of Illinois, Nebraska, and the Dakotas, it is called the Township, only a variation of name from the "town," and having the same origin.

In California it is called the Judicial Township, and in parts of the Dakotas it is called the School Township.

In Alabama, Colorado, Florida, Idaho, Oregon, Utah, Washington, and parts of Illinois and Nebraska, it is called the Election Precinct, from the fact that it was the subdivision made for the convenience of voters.

In Georgia it is called the Militia District, from the fact that each subdivision furnished a certain proportionate number of men for the militia service of the

State.

In Kentucky, Virginia, and West Virginia, it is called the Magisterial District, from the fact that it was constituted as the limit of the jurisdiction of a local magistrate.

In Louisiana it is called the Police Jury Ward, perhaps for the reason that from each one of these subdivisions a warden was elected to administer the parish government.

In Maryland and Wyoming it is called the Election District, from the fact that it was the subdivision made for the convenience of voters.

In Tennessee it is called the Civil District--probably, next to "town" or "township," the most fitting name for the smallest subdivision of civil government.

In Texas it is called the Justice's Precinct, as being the limit of a justice's jurisdiction.

In some of the New England States, also, districts which have not the entire town organization are provisionally called Plantations or Grants, being subject to the administration, in some local affairs, of other towns.

But under whatever name the civil unit may exist, it is the primary seat of government. In many cases the original reason for the name has disappeared, while the character of the government has greatly changed, and been modified and developed from the first crude forms.

THREE GENERAL CLASSES.--As a result, there are at present but three general classes into which we need subdivide the civil unit in the various States: these are the Civil District, which would include the "Beat," "Hundred," "Election Precinct," "Militia District," and numerous other classes, embracing about one half the States of the Union; the Town, which has its fullest development in the New England States; and the Township, which in some States has nearly the full development of a New England town, while in other States it has a looser organisation, approximating the civil district of the Southern and Southwestern States.

# THE CIVIL DISTRICT, PROPER.

We shall treat of the various forms of the civil unit which we have classed under the general name of civil district before we speak of the town and the township, because they are simpler and much less developed, and therefore naturally constitute the simplest form of the civil unit.

NUMBER, SIZE.--In number and size, civil districts vary widely in different States and in different counties of the same State. There are rarely less than five or more than twelve districts to the county.

PURPOSES.--The division of the county into districts, each with its own court of law, brings justice to the people's doors. It secures officers to every part of the county, thus affording better means for the punishment of crimes. It provides a speedy trial for minor offences and minor suits. It aids the higher courts by relieving them of a multitude of small cases. As each district has one or more polling-places, it secures convenience to the electors in casting their votes.

GOVERNMENT.--The functions of the civil district are judicial and executive, and lie within a narrow range. Its government possesses no legislative or corporate power whatever; it can not make a single law, however unimportant. Within a narrow jurisdiction or sphere, it applies the law to particular cases, and this is the chief purpose for its existence. Whenever the civil unit possesses more powers than are herein set forth, it is more properly described under the township in the next chapter, no matter what name it may go by locally.

## CITIZENS.

The citizens of the civil district are the people residing within it. It exists for their benefit, that they may be secure in life, liberty, and property. In a certain sense they constitute the district, since its government concerns them directly, and others only remotely.

RIGHTS.--All citizens have a right to the full and equal protection of the laws. Each has a right to be secure in his person and property; to demand that the peace be preserved; to do all things according to his own will, provided he does not trespass upon the rights of others. No one in the family, in the school, in the civil district, in the county, in the State, or in the nation, has the right to do or say any thing which interferes with the life, liberty, property, or happiness of another. Any act which interferes with the rights of others is an offence against the common good and against the law. It is chiefly for the prevention and punishment of these unlawful acts that the civil district exists, with its court and its officers.

All legal voters of the district have the right to participate in its government by exercising a free choice in the selection of its officers, except in States where these officers are appointed. They have the right to cast their votes without fear or favor. This is one of the most important and sacred rights that freemen possess. Free government can not exist without it. The law guarantees it, and all the power of the State may be employed to maintain it. Therefore, whoever prevents a voter from exercising the right of suffrage does it at his own peril.

DUTIES.--As the citizens of the civil district have rights, they also have corresponding duties. As they may demand protection and the preservation of the peace, so it is their duty to obey the law and assist the officers in its enforcement, in order that the same protection may be extended to the whole people. Each should abstain from acts that injure others, and render cheerful aid to all in securing their rights through the law.

All qualified voters have the right, and it is also their duty, to vote. The voters elect the officers of the district, and are therefore its rulers. When they fail to vote, they fail to rule--fail in their duty to the people and to themselves. The duty to vote implies the duty to vote right, to vote for good men and for good measures. Therefore, citizens should study their duty as voters, that they may elect honest, capable, faithful officers, and support the parties and principles that will best promote the good of the country? Every one should study his political duty with the best light that he can obtain, decide what is right, and then vote his sentiments honestly and fearlessly. If the district has good government, the voters deserve the credit; if it has bad government, the voters deserve the blame.

OFFICERS.

The officers of the district are the justices of the peace and the constable. In some States there is only one justice to each district, in other States there are two, and in others there are three.

JUSTICE OF THE PEACE.--The office of justice of the peace is one of dignity and importance. Justices can render great service to society by the proper discharge of their duties. They may have much to do with enforcing the law, and therefore the best men should be elected to this office.

ELECTION, TERM OF OFFICE.--Justices of the peace are usually elected by the qualified voters of the district. In some States the governor appoints them. The term of office is two, three, four, or even seven years, varying in different States.

DUTIES.--The duties of justices of the peace are principally judicial, and their jurisdiction extends throughout the county. Upon the sworn statement of the person making complaint, they issue warrants for the arrest of offenders. With the aid of juries, they hold court for the trial of minor offences--such as the breach of the peace--punishable by fine or brief imprisonment. They sometimes try those charged with higher crimes, and acquit; or, if the proof is sufficient, remand the accused to trial by a higher court. This is called an examining trial. They try civil suits where the amount involved does not exceed a fixed amount--fifty dollars in some States, and one hundred dollars in others--and prevent crime by requiring reckless persons to give security to keep the peace. Justices sometimes preside, instead of the coroner, at inquests, and in some States they have important duties as officers of the county.

CONSTABLE, ELECTION, TERM OF OFFICE.--There is usually one constable--in some States more--in each civil district. Constables, like the justices, are elected in most States; but in some they are appointed. The term of office is usually the same as that of the justice in the same State.

DUTIES.--The constable is termed a ministerial officer because it is his duty to minister to, or wait upon, the justice's court. He serves warrants, writs, and other processes of the justice, and sometimes those of higher courts. He preserves the public peace, makes arrests for its violation, and in some States collects the taxes apportioned to his civil district.

SUGGESTIVE QUESTIONS.

1. In what respect does civil government differ from family or school government?

2. Why does the government of the civil district concern its people directly and others remotely?

3. What is meant by the civil unit? By what names is it known in the various States?

4. What are the three general classes under which the civil unit may be considered?

5. Why can not free government exist without the right to vote?

6. Why should the people try to secure their rights through the law?

7. What is the purpose of the subdivision of a county into districts?

8. Define in general terms the rights and duties of the citizens of civil districts.

9. By what other names are justices of the peace sometimes called?

10. Why is the jurisdiction of a justice's court limited?

11. Who are the justices of this civil district?

12. When elected, and what is their term of office?

13. Who is constable of this district?

QUESTION FOR DEBATE.

Resolved, That the government of the civil district should have a legislative department.

CHAPTER IV.

THE TOWNSHIP OR TOWN.

INTRODUCTION.--We have learned that in the Southern States the civil unit under various names may be described under the common name of the civil district; that in the New England States it is called the town, and in many of the Western States it is known as the township. As the powers and functions of the town and the township are the same in kind, differing only in extent, and as the two names are so often used, the one for the other, we shall consider both under the head of the township.

As a rule, the township possesses more extensive governmental functions in the Eastern than in the Western States, and in the West it possesses functions much more extensive than those of the civil district in the South. Many of the most important powers that belong to the county in the Southern States belong to the township in the Eastern and the Western States.

FORMATION.--In the Eastern States the townships were formed in the first settlement of the country, and afterward a number of townships were combined to form the county. In the Western States the townships were surveyed, and their boundaries marked, by agents of the general government, before the Territories became States of the Union. As a natural result, the townships of the Eastern States are irregular in shape and size, while those of the Western States have a regular form, each being about six miles square. In the Western States the township is usually composed of thirty-six sections, each section being one mile square, and containing six hundred and forty acres of land.

PURPOSES.--It is an old and true maxim that government should be brought as near the people as possible. This the township system does. In our country all power resides in the people, and the township provides a convenient means of ascertaining their wishes and of executing their will. The farther away the government, the less will be the people's power; the nearer the government, the greater will be the people's power. The township system enables each community to attend to its own local affairs--a work which no other agency can do so well--to remove readily and speedily its local public grievances, and to obtain readily and speedily its local public needs.

## CITIZENS.

The citizens of the township are the people living in it, whether native or foreigners who have become citizens. It exists for their benefit, to afford them a means of securing their rights and of redressing their wrongs. It is these persons that the law has in view when setting forth the privileges and immunities of citizenship.

RIGHTS.--All citizens of the township arc entitled to enjoy the rights of "life, liberty, property, and the pursuit of happiness." The township government exists for the purpose of securing these rights to the people. All have equal claims to the fullest protection of the law. They may use their own property as they choose, and do whatever pleases them, so long as they do not interfere with the rights of others. Whenever one's act, speech, or property interferes with the rights of others, he falls under the censure of the law and becomes subject to its penalty.

All male inhabitants born in the United States, and foreigners who have become citizens, who have resided within the State, county, and township the time required by law, are entitled to vote at all township, county, state, and national elections. Several States require ability to read, or the payment of poll-tax, as a qualification to vote; a few permit the subjects of foreign countries to vote; and in some States women are permitted to vote in school elections or in all elections. Lunatics, idiots, paupers, and persons convicted of certain high crimes are disfranchised; that is, are not permitted to vote. The right of suffrage is one of great power and value, being the basis of all free government, and is jealously guarded by the laws of the land.

DUTIES.--The people have extensive rights and they have equally extensive duties. Each citizen has rights that others must respect. It is the duty of each to observe and regard the rights of all other persons; and when he does not, the law interferes by its officers and deprives him of his own rights by fine or imprisonment, and in some instances by a still more severe penalty. It is the duty of the people to love and serve the country; to be good citizens; to labor for the public good; to obey the law, and to assist the officers in its enforcement.

It is the duty of the qualified voters to give the township good government by electing good officers. A vote cast for a bad man or a bad measure is an attack upon the rights of every person in the community. The power of suffrage is held for the public good; but it is used for the public injury when incompetent or unfaithful men are elected to office. Good government and the happiness and prosperity of the country depend upon an honest and intelligent vote.

## GOVERNMENT.

The township government possesses legislative, judicial, and executive functions. It has a legislative department to make local laws, a judicial department to apply the laws to particular cases, and an executive department to enforce these and other laws. The three functions are of nearly equal prominence in the Eastern States, but in the West the executive function is more prominent than the legislative and the judicial.

CORPORATE POWER.--Each township is a corporation; that is, in any business affair it may act as a single person. In its corporate capacity it can sue and be sued; borrow money; buy, rent, and sell property for public purposes. When it is said that the township possesses these powers, it is meant that the people of the township, acting as a single political body, possess them.

OFFICERS.--The officers of the township are more numerous, and their functions are more extensive than those of the civil district. Many officers are the same in name, and others have the same duties as those of the county in the Southern States.

LEGISLATIVE DEPARTMENT; THE PEOPLE.--In the Eastern States the legislative department of the township government has more extensive functions than in the West. In the New England States most local affairs belong to the township government, and the county is of minor importance. In these and a few other States the people make their own local laws instead of delegating this power to representatives. The electors of the township meet annually at a fixed place, upon a day appointed by law, discuss questions of public concern, elect the township officers, levy township taxes, make appropriations of money for public purposes, fix the salaries and hear the reports of officers, and decide upon a course of action for the coming year. Thus the people themselves, or more strictly speaking, the qualified voters, are the government. In some States special town meetings may be called for special purposes. The town meeting places local public affairs under the direct control of the people, and thus gives them a personal interest in the government, and makes them feel a personal responsibility for its acts. Another benefit of the system is that it trains the people to deal with political matters, and so prepares them to act intelligently in all the affairs of the State and the nation.

In the Western States the county government is more important, and township legislation is confined to a narrow range. In power and importance the township of most Western States is intermediate between the town of the East and the civil district of the South.

SELECTMEN OR TRUSTEES.--The legislative power of the township is vested in the trustees, town council, or selectmen, as they are variously termed. The number of trustees or selectmen is not the same in all parts of the Union, being fixed at three in most States of the West, and varying in New England with the wishes of the electors. The trustees, councilmen, or selectmen are elected by the qualified voters of the township for a term of one, two, or three years, varying in different States. They are the legal guardians of the public interests of the township, and make laws or ordinances, sometimes called by-laws, expressly pertaining to the local wants of the community, and to a limited extent may levy taxes.

In some States, especially those of the East, the principal duties of the trustees or selectmen are executive. They divide the township into road districts; open roads on petition; select jurors; build and repair bridges and town halls, where the expenditure is small; act as judges of elections; purchase and care for cemeteries; have charge of the poor not in the county charge; and act for the township in its corporate capacity. If any thing goes wrong in the public affairs of the town, complaint is made to these officers.

EXECUTIVE DEPARTMENT.--Most of the public affairs of the township, as well as of all other governments, pertain to the executive department. Its duties are far more extensive, and its officers are more numerous, than those of the other departments. The executive officers of the township are the clerk, the treasurer, the school directors, the assessor, the supervisors, and the constables. In most States all these officers are elected by the qualified voters; but in some the clerk, the treasurer, and the constables are elected by the town council.

CLERK.--The clerk of the township is clerk of the trustees, council, or selectmen, and in some States of the school board. He attends the meetings of the trustees, and makes a careful record of the proceedings. He keeps the poll-lists and other legal papers of the township, administers oaths, and notifies officers of their election. In the New England States, and some others, he keeps a record of the marriages, births, and deaths, calls the town meeting to order, reads the warrant under which it is held, presides until a moderator is chosen, and then acts as clerk of the meeting.

TREASURER.--Taxes collected from the people for local purposes are paid to the treasurer. He receives all fines, forfeitures, and license-fees paid to the township. He is the keeper of the township funds, giving bond for the faithful performance of his duties, and pays out money upon the written order of the trustees, attested by the clerk. In some States, as in New York, there is no separate township treasurer, the above and other duties being performed by the supervisor, who is the chief officer of the township.

SCHOOL DIRECTORS.--The school directors have charge of the public schools of the township. The number of directors varies widely, being usually three, five, or more. In a few of the States, the clerks of the district trustees constitute the township school directors, or township board of education. The directors levy taxes for school purposes, visit and inspect the public schools, adopt text-books, regulate the order of studies and length of the term, fix salaries, purchase furniture and apparatus, and make reports to the higher school officers. In some States they examine teachers and grant certificates to teach. In many States a part of these duties falls to the county superintendent.

ASSESSOR.--The assessor makes a list of the names of all persons subject to taxation, estimates the value of their real and personal property, assesses a tax thereon, and in some States delivers this list to the auditor, and in others to the collector of taxes. In most States there, is also a poll-tax of from one to three dollars, sometimes more, laid upon all male inhabitants more than twenty-one years of age. In some States there are two or more assessors to the township, and in others real estate is valued only once in ten years.

COMMISSIONERS, or surveyors of highways, have charge of the

construction and repair of highways, summon those subject to labor on the road, and direct their work.

SUPERVISOR.--In some States the chief executive duties of the town fall upon the supervisor, but his principal duties are rather as a member of the county board of supervisors.

CONSTABLES.--Constables are ministerial and police officers. There are usually two or three in each township. They wait upon the justice's court, and are subject to his orders. They preserve the public peace, serve warrants and other processes, and in some States act as collectors of taxes.

COLLECTOR, ETC.--In some States the township has a collector and three or more auditors. They are usually elected by the trustees, or council, but in a few of the States they are elected by the town meeting. The collector collects the township taxes, giving bond for the faithful performance of his duties. In order to secure honesty and efficiency in public office, and to exhibit the financial condition of the township, the auditors annually examine the books of the treasurer and the collector, and publish a report showing the receipts and expenditures of public money.

In a few States the township has a field-driver and a pound-keeper, whose respective duties are to take stray animals to the pound, an enclosure kept for the purpose, and to retain them with good care until the owner is notified and pays all expenses; two or more fence-viewers, who decide disputes about fences; surveyors of lumber, who measure and mark lumber offered for sale; and sealers, who test and certify weights and measures used in trade. These officers are usually appointed by the selectmen.

JUDICIAL DEPARTMENT; JUSTICES.--The judicial power is vested in the justices, who are elected by the qualified voters of the town. There are usually two or three justices, but in some States there is only one in each township. The term of office is one, two, three, four, or more years, varying in different States. Justices preside in the justice's court to hear and determine suits at law. "This is the humblest court in the land, the court of greatest antiquity, and the court upon which all other courts are founded."[1] The justice's court tries petty offences and civil suits for small amounts. In some States the justices preside at the town meetings, and in others they perform the duties of coroner in the township.

[1]Thorpe's Civil Government.

SUGGESTIVE QUESTIONS.

1. Has this State the township system? If so, give the name and number of your township.

2. How does the township system provide a convenient means of ascertaining and of executing the people's will?

3. Why is the people's power greater when the government is near?

4. Why can the community manage its own affairs better than any other agency can manage them?

5. How do people secure their rights?

6. What is meant by falling under the censure of the law?

7. What is a naturalized person?

8. Is it right for subjects of foreign governments to vote? Why?

9. Is it right for women to vote?

10. Why is suffrage the basis of all free government?

11. What is a more severe penalty than imprisonment?

12. How can people serve the country?

13. What is a good citizen?

14. Why is a bad vote an attack on the rights of the people?

15. What other laws than those made by the legislative department of the

township does the executive department enforce?

16. How do you like the New England town meeting? Why?

17. Name some duties that belong to the executive department.

18. What is a poll-list?

19. What are the duties of judges of election?

20. Of what use is a record of marriages, births, and deaths?

21. What is meant by license-fees?

22. What persons are subject to taxation?

23. What is a poll-tax, and is it right? Why?

24. Who are subject to road duty in this State?

25. Give the names of the officers of this township.

QUESTION FOR DEBATE.

Resolved, That the town meeting is the best system of local government yet devised.

CHAPTER V

THE COUNTY.

INTRUDUCTORY.--The county is a political division of the State, and is composed of civil districts or of townships. It bears the name of county in all parts of the country except in Louisiana, where a similar organization is known as a parish. In New England the county has less power than the town; in the Western States it has more than the township; and in the Southern States it has far more than the civil district, being there the unit of political influence.

PURPOSES.--The county organization brings justice near the people, enables them to attend to local affairs too extensive for a smaller community, and affords a medium by which they may transact business with the State. It serves as a convenient basis of apportioning members of the legislature among the people. It maintains local officers, such as sheriff and prosecuting attorney, whose duties would be too narrow if confined to a township. It secures a competent and higher tribunal than the justice's court for the trial of suits at law. This was the original purpose, and is still the controlling reason for the division of the States into counties.

FORMATION, AREA.--Counties are formed, their rights are conferred, and their duties imposed, by act of the State legislature. In most States counties vary greatly in shape and size, but in some of the Western States they have a regular form. The average area of counties in the United States is eight hundred and thirty square miles; the average area of those east of the Mississippi River is only three hundred and eighty square miles.

COUNTY SEAT.--The county government resides at the county seat, county town, or shire town, as it is variously called. The court-house, the jail, the public offices, and sometimes other county buildings are located at the county seat. Here are kept the records of the courts; also, usually copies of the deeds, wills, mortgages, and other important papers of the people.

COUNTY GOVERNMENT.

The county, like the United States, the State, and the township, has a republican form of government; that is, it is governed by representatives elected by the people. In nearly all States the county government has three departments, legislative, executive, and judicial; but the functions of making, of executing, and of explaining the laws, are not always kept separate and distinct. In a few States the county does not have a judicial department.

OFFICERS.--County officers and township officers have duties similar in kind, but the former have charge of the larger interests. The usual officers of the county are the commissioners or supervisors, the county attorney or prosecuting attorney, the county superintendent of schools or school commissioner, the sheriff, the treasurer, the auditor, the county clerk or common pleas clerk, the surveyor, the coroner, and the county judge and surrogate, or probate judge. In the counties of many States one or more of these officers are lacking, and others have different names from those here given. In the Western and the Southern States county officers are elected by the direct vote of the people; in most of the New England States some of them are chosen in other ways. The terms of county officers vary in different parts of the Union, being usually two, three, or four years; but in some States certain officers are elected for a longer term.

LEGISLATIVE DEPARTMENT: COUNTY COMMISSIONERS, OR BOARD OF SUPERVISORS.--In most States the public interests of the county are intrusted to a board of officers, three or five in number, called county commissioners. In some States the board consists of one or more supervisors from each township, and is called the board of supervisors. In a few States the board consists of all the justices of the county, with the county judge as presiding officer.

The county commissioners, or board of supervisors, have charge of the county property, such as the court-house, the jail, and the county infirmary; make orders and raise funds for the erection of county buildings, and for the construction and improvement of highways and bridges; provide polling-places; make appropriations of money for public purposes; and act as the chief agents of the county in its corporate capacity. In some States they fix the salaries of county officers; in others they have power to form new townships and to change the township boundaries. In several States the functions of the board are almost wholly executive.

EXECUTIVE DEPARTMENT: COUNTY ATTORNEYS, OR PROSECUTIN ATTORNEYS.--The county attorney, or prosecuting attorney, is the county's counsellor at law, and when requested gives legal advice to all the county officers. It is his duty to prosecute the accused in the trial of crimes and offences, in the justice's court, the county court, and in some States in the circuit court or district court; to represent the county in all civil suits to which it is a party; and to act for it in all cases in which its legal interests are involved.

COUNTY SUPERINDENTENT OF SCHOOLS.--In some States there is no county superintendent of schools. In most States there is such an officer elected by the township school directors or by the people of the county, or appointed by the State superintendent of public instruction. In a few States the county is divided into two or more districts, each having a commissioner of schools.

The county superintendent, or school commissioner, is the chief school officer of the county. He administers the public school system, condemns unfit school-houses and orders others built, examines teachers and grants certificates, holds teachers' institutes, visits and directs the schools, instructs teachers in their duties, interests the people in education, and reports the condition of the schools to the State superintendent of public instruction. He is one of the most important officers of the county, a capable administration of his duties being of the greatest benefit to the whole people.

SHERIFF.--"The sheriff is the guardian of the peace of the county and the executive officer of its courts."[1] He preserves the peace, arrests persons charged with crime, serves writs and other processes in both civil and criminal cases, makes proclamation of all elections, summons jurors, and ministers to the courts of his county. In States having no county jailer, the sheriff has charge of the prisons and prisoners, and is responsible for their safe-keeping. When persons refuse to pay their taxes, he seizes and sells enough property to pay the sum assessed; and in some States he is the collector of all State and county revenue.

COUNTY TREASURER.--The duties of the treasurer are indicated by the title of his office. He receives all county taxes, licenses, and other money paid into the county treasury. In most States he is custodian of the county's financial records, and of the tax-collector's books, and in others he collects all the taxes assessed in the county. He gives bond for the faithful performance of his duties, and pays out funds upon the warrant of the county commissioners. In most States having no county treasurer, the sheriff is keeper of the public money.

AUDITOR.--The auditor is the guardian of the county's financial interests. He examines the books and papers of officers who receive or disburse county funds; keeps a record of receipts and expenditures; draws all warrants for the payment of public money; and publishes a report of the county's financial transactions. In some States he receives the assessor's returns, apportions taxes among the people, and prepares the tax-collector's duplicate list. In States having no county auditor, these duties are performed by other officers.

COUNTY CLERK, OR COMMON PLEAS CLERK.--The county clerk, or common pleas clerk, is the recording officer of the county court, or probate court, and in some States of the circuit court. He issues writs, preserves papers, and records judgments. In many States he issues licenses, preserves election returns, and records wills, deeds, mortgages, and other important papers.

RECORDER, OR REGISTER.--In many States the county has a recorder, or register, instead of the county clerk, and in some States it has both. The recorder, or register, makes a record in books kept for that purpose, of wills, deeds, mortgages, village plats, and powers of attorney. Some of these instruments must be recorded in order to make them valid in law. In some States having no recorder, these duties are performed by the township clerk, and in others by the county clerk.

SURVEYOR.--The county surveyor, or engineer, surveys tracts of land to locate lines, determine areas, and to settle conflicting claims. In some States his services are frequently needed in the transfer of real estate. In most States he makes plots of surveys, issues maps of the county, and has charge of the construction of roads and bridges.

CORONER.--The coroner investigates the death of persons who have died by violence, or in prison, or from causes unknown. He receives notice of the death; a jury is summoned; witnesses testify; and the jury renders a verdict in writing, stating the cause and the manner of the death. This inquiry is known as the coroner's inquest. In some States when the office of sheriff is vacant, the coroner performs the duties.

OTHER OFFICERS.--In some States there are superintendents of the poor, or infirmary directors, who have charge of the county infirmary in which the dependent poor are maintained; in others the township overseers of the poor support these unfortunates with funds furnished for that purpose by the county. In some States there is a collector who collects all the taxes of the county; a county jailer who holds prisoners in custody and has charge of the county buildings, under the commissioners' directions; and also a circuit clerk, or district clerk, who is the recording officer of the circuit court, or district court as it is often called.

JUDICIAL DEPARTMENT: COUNTY JUDGE OR PROBATE JUDGE.--

The judicial power of the county is vested in the county judge, or probate judge, who in many States is its most prominent and important officer. He has jurisdiction of wills and estates, appoints administrators and guardians, and settles their accounts. In many states he grants licenses; presides over the legislative body of the county; makes orders opening roads and appointing overseers of the public highway: appoints officers of elections; holds examining trials; sits in the county court to try minor offences and civil suits for small amounts; and in a few States acts as county superintendent of schools.

In some States there is a probate judge, or judge of the orphan's court, in addition to the county judge.

[1]Thorpe's Civil Government.

SUGGESTIVE QUESTIONS.

1. What is meant by unit of political influence?

2. What affairs are too extensive for a smaller community than the county?

3. Why is the county seat so called?

4. State the terms and the names of the officers of this county.

5. Why do the officers of the county need legal advice?

6. What is meant by the sheriff administering to the courts?

7. What are licenses?

8. Of what use is the treasurer's bond?

9. What is the collector's duplicate list?

10. What is a writ?

11. What is the plot of a survey?

12. What is a will? an administrator?

13. What is an examining trial?

14. Do you think the county judge or probate judge should act as superintendent of schools? Why?

QUESTION FOR DEBATE.

Resolved, That a poll-tax is unjust.

CHAPTER VI.

MUNICIPAL CORPORATIONS.

VILLAGES, BOROUGHS, AND CITIES.--The county usually has within its limits villages or cities, organized under separate and distinct governments. When the people become so thickly settled that the township and county government do not meet their local public wants, the community is incorporated as a village. Villages are often called towns, and incorporated as such, especially in the Southern States; but the word taken in this sense must not be confounded with the same word, denoting a political division of the county in New England, New York, and Wisconsin.

THE VILLAGE, OR BOROUGH.

INCORPORATION.--In most States, villages, boroughs, and towns are incorporated under general laws made by the State legislature. A majority of the legal voters living within the proposed limits must first vote in favor of the proposition to incorporate. In some States, villages are incorporated by special act of the legislature.

GOVERNMENT PURPOSES.--The purposes of the village or borough government are few in number, and lie within a narrow limit. It is a corporate body, having the usual corporate powers. Under the village organization, local public works, such as streets, sidewalks, and bridges, are maintained more readily and in better condition than under the government, of the township and county. The presence of the village officers tends to preserve the peace and make crime less frequent.

OFFICERS.--The usual officers of the village or borough are the trustees or councilmen, whose duties are mostly legislative; the marshal, and sometimes a president or mayor; a collector and a treasurer, whose duties are executive; and the recorder, or police judge, or justices of the peace, whose duties are judicial. The officers are usually elected by the legal voters, and serve for a term of one or two years. In many villages the president and the collector are elected by the trustees, the former from among their own number.

DUTIES.--The trustees or council pass laws, called ordinances, relating to streets, fast driving, lamps, water-works, the police system, public parks, public health, and the public buildings. They appoint minor officers, such as clerk, regular and special policemen, keeper of the cemetery, and fire-wardens; prescribe the duties, and fix the compensation of these officers.

The president or mayor is the chief executive officer, and is charged with seeing that the laws are enforced. In villages having no president or mayor, this duty devolves upon the trustees. The marshal is a ministerial officer, with the same duties and often the same jurisdiction as the constable, and is sometimes known by that name. He preserves the peace, makes arrests, serves processes, and waits upon the recorder's court. The collector collects the village taxes. The treasurer receives all village funds, and pays out money upon the order of the trustees.

The recorder or police judge tries minor offences, such as breach of the peace, and holds examining trials of higher crimes. His jurisdiction is usually equal to that of justices of the peace in the same State. In some States the village has two justices of the peace instead of the recorder, these being also officers of the county.

THE CITY.

When the village, borough, or town becomes so large that its government does not meet the people's local public needs, it is incorporated as a city. Where the country is sparsely settled the peace is seldom broken, private interests do not conflict, the people's public needs are small, and therefore the functions of government are few and light. As the population grows dense, the public peace is oftener disturbed, crime increases, disputes about property arise, the public needs become numerous and important, and the officers of the law must interfere to preserve order and protect the people. The fewer the people to the square mile, the fewer and lighter are the functions of government; the more people to the square mile, the more and stronger must be the functions of government.

INCORPORATION.--Cities and villages or boroughs differ principally in size and in the scope of their corporate authority. A city is larger in area and population, and the powers and privileges of its government are more extensive. In most States cities may be incorporated under general laws, but some cities are incorporated by special acts of the State legislature. The act or deed of incorporation is called the city charter. The charter names the city, fixes its limits, erects it as a distinct political corporation, sets forth its powers and privileges, names its officers, prescribes their duties, and authorizes the city to act as an independent government. The legislature may amend the charter at any time, and the acts and laws of the city must not conflict with the constitution of the State or of the United States.

WARDS.--The city is usually divided into wards for convenience in executing the laws, and especially in electing representatives in the city government. Wards vary greatly in area and population, and their number depends in a measure upon the size of the city. Each usually elects a member of the board of education, and one or more members of each branch of the city council. Each ward is subdivided into precincts for convenience in establishing polling-places.

CITY INSTITUTIONS.--Cities maintain a number of institutions, peculiar to themselves, for the public welfare. The frequency of destructive fires causes the formation of a fire department. A police force must be organized to protect life and property. A system of sewerage is necessary to the public health. There must be gas-works or electric-light works, that the streets may be lighted, and water-works to supply water for public and private use. In many cities gas-works and water-works are operated by private parties or by private corporations.

FINANCES.--Each city has an independent financial system, which requires skillful management. The city borrows money, issuing interest-bearing bonds in payment, and engages in extensive public improvements. The large outlays for paving the streets, constructing water-works, laying out parks, erecting public buildings, and for maintaining police systems and fire departments, cause cities to incur debts often amounting to many millions of dollars. As the result of the greater expense of its government, and as its people also pay State and county taxes, the rate of taxation in a city is far greater than in rural districts and villages.

CITIZENS: RIGHTS AND DUTIES.--The qualifications, the rights, and the duties of citizens of the city are the same as those of citizens of the township and the county. The qualifications of voters are also usually the same. The duties of voters are the same in all elections, whether in the school district, the civil district, the city, the county, the State, or the United States; namely, to vote for the best men and the best measures. Under whatever division of government the people are living, they always have the same interest in the maintenance of order, in the enforcement of the laws, in the triumph of right, principles, and in the election of good men to office.

GOVERNMENT.--A city often has a more complex government than that of the State in which the city is situated. The massing of so many people, representing so many interests, requires a government with strong legislative, executive, and judicial functions. One of the great questions of our time is how to secure economy and efficiency in city government; and, as our cities are growing with great rapidity, the problem is daily becoming more difficult to solve.

OFFICERS.--The legislative power is vested in the city council, in many cases composed of a board of aldermen and of a common council. The executive authority is vested in the mayor, the city attorney or solicitor, the city clerk, the assessor, the collector, the treasurer, the city engineer or surveyor, the board of public works, the street commissioner, the school board or board of education, and the superintendent of schools. The judicial power is vested in the city court, police court, or recorder's court, as it is variously termed; in a number of justices' courts; and in the higher courts, which are also courts of the county in which the city is located. The officers of the city are usually elected by the legal voters, but in some cities the collector, the city engineer, the street commissioner, and a number of subordinate officers are appointed by the mayor or city council. The superintendent of schools is elected by the school board.

DUTIES.--In many small cities, and in several of the larger cities, such as New York, Chicago, and San Francisco, the council consists only of the board of aldermen. When the council is composed of two branches, a law can not be made by one of them alone; it must be passed by both; and if vetoed by the mayor, it must be passed again, and in most cities by a two thirds vote, or it is void. The council makes laws, or ordinances, regulating the police force; fixing the rate of city taxation; ordering the issue of bonds and the construction of public works; and making appropriations for public purposes.

The mayor is the chief executive of the city. It is his duty to see that the laws are enforced. He appoints a number of subordinate officers, and in most cities may veto the acts of the city council. The duties of the city attorney, the city clerk, the assessor, the collector, the treasurer, the school board, and the superintendent of schools are similar to those of township and county officers of the same name. The city engineer has charge of the construction of sewers and the improvement of parks. The street commissioner attends to the construction and repair of the streets, crossings, and sidewalks. There are a number of officers appointed by the mayor or the council, such as chief of police, chief of the fire department, and the city physician, who have duties connected with their special departments.

The city judge, police judge, or recorder, has duties similar to those of the same officer in an incorporated village. Cities also have higher courts, variously named, whose judges have duties and jurisdiction equivalent to those of county officers of the same grade. Because offenses against the law are more frequent, officers are more numerous in cities than in the rural districts.

COMMISSION PLAN OF CITY GOVERNMENT.--In recent times the "commission plan" of government has been adopted for many cities, in a number of different States. This plan gives full control of the city government and its minor officials to a commission or council composed of a few men (usually five) elected by the voters of the whole city. This commission exercises both legislative and executive functions. It is composed of a mayor, and councilmen or commissioners who act also as heads of administrative departments.

RECALL.--In a few States a mayor or councilman (or other local or State officer elected by the people) may be displaced before the expiration of his term of office. If a sufficient number of voters petition to have this done, a new election is held to decide whether he or some one else shall have the office for the rest of the term.

SUGGESTIVE QUESTIONS.

1. What is meant by incorporating a village?

2. What is a breach of the peace?

3. What are polling-places?

4. To what State officer does the mayor of a city or town correspond?

5. Why are offenses against the laws more frequent in the cities than in the rural districts?

6. What is the largest city of this State? Is its council composed of one body or of two?

QUESTION FOR DEBATE.

Resolved, That the legislative department of a city government should consist of only one deliberative body.

CHAPTER VII.

THE STATE.

INTRODUCTORY.--After the county, the government nearest us is that of the State. The political divisions which we have considered are subject to the State, holding their powers as grants from its government. The State can make and unmake them, and we owe them obedience because the State has commanded it. As we sometimes express it, the sovereignty or supreme sway of these local divisions resides in the State.

DEFINITION.--A State is a community of free citizens living within a territory with fixed limits, governed by laws based upon a constitution of their own adoption, and possessing all governmental powers not granted to the United States. Each State is a republic and maintains a republican form of government, which is guaranteed by the United States. The State is supreme within its own sphere, but its authority must not conflict with that of the national government. A State is sometimes called a commonwealth because it binds the whole people together for their common weal or common good.

FORMATION OF ORIGINAL STATES.--The thirteen original colonies were principally settled by people from Europe. The colonial rights were set forth and boundaries fixed by charters granted by the crown of England. In the Declaration of Independence these colonies declared themselves "free and independent States." After the treaty of peace which acknowledged their independence, they framed and adopted the national constitution, and thereby became the United States of America.

ADMISSION OF NEW STATES.--New States are admitted into the Union by special acts of the Congress of the United States. An organized Territory having the necessary population sends a memorial to Congress asking to be admitted as a State. Congress then passes a law called an "enabling act," authorizing the people of the Territory to form a State constitution. When the people have framed and adopted a State constitution not in conflict with the Constitution of the United States, Congress passes another act admitting the new State into the Union "upon an equal footing with the original States in all respects whatever." Sometimes the enabling act provides for admission on proclamation of the President of the United States. Several of the Territories adopted State constitutions and were admitted as States without enabling acts.

PURPOSES.--The State keeps power near the people, and thus makes them more secure in their liberty. "The powers not granted to the United States, nor prohibited to the States, are reserved to the States respectively or to the people." If the whole country were a single republic without State divisions, power would be withdrawn from the people and become centralized in the national government.

Our political system leaves the various functions of government to the smallest political communities that can perform them efficiently. The county has charge of all public interests that can be managed by it as well as by the State. Many public affairs, such as popular education,[1] private corporations, and the organization of the smaller political divisions, can be better managed by the State than by the National Government, and are therefore properly left to the State's direction.

Parts of the country widely separated differ in climate and soil, giving rise to different industries and occupations, which require different laws, made and administered by different States. The State serves as a convenient basis for the apportionment of members of both houses of Congress, and State institutions preserve and develop the local individuality and self-reliance of the people.

FUNCTIONS.--The functions of the State are very extensive, including the greater part of those acts of government which preserve society by affording security to life, liberty, property, and the pursuit of happiness.

The State government touches the citizens at most points; that is, all those laws that concern the body of the people in their ordinary daily life are made and enforced by the State, or by the smaller political divisions of the State, acting under the State's directions. Officers discharge their duties, arrests are made, courts are held, offenders are punished, justice is meted out, and taxes are collected, by the authority of the State.

The National Government has similar functions to perform in every part of the country, but they are far less frequent than those of the State.

INSTITUTIONS.--The State maintains a number of charitable and other institutions for the public welfare. It makes appropriations of land or money for the support of asylums, prisons, reformatories, scientific institutions, schools, colleges, and universities. The support of these institutions, the payment of salaries, the administration of justice, and the conduct of other public interests, involve large annual expenditures, often amounting to several millions of dollars.

CITIZENS.

The citizens of a State are the people who live in it, whether natives of the United States, or foreigners who have been adopted. Persons who are citizens of the United States are thereby citizens of the State in which they reside. They have all the rights that freemen can possess, and enjoy a larger freedom than do the people of any other country.

The legal voters, often called electors, are the male citizens who have resided in the State, the county, and the township, or voting precinct, the time required by law to entitle them to vote. The length of residence required in the State varies, being two years in some, six months in others, and one year in most States. Several States permit citizens of foreign countries to vote, and a few permit women to vote.

RIGHTS.--Every citizen has the right to be secure in his person; to be free from attack and annoyance; to go when and where he may choose; to keep, enjoy, and dispose of his property; and to provide in his own way for the welfare of himself and of those dependent upon him.

The rights of the people are set forth at length and with great precision in a portion of the State constitution called the Bill of Rights. These rights must be exercised under the restrictions of the law, and with due regard for the same rights held by others.

The legal voters have the right to vote in all local, State, and national elections. They are voters in national elections by virtue of being voters in State elections. The right to vote implies the right to be voted for, and the right to hold office; but for many officers the State requires a longer residence and other qualifications than those prescribed for voters.

DUTIES.--For every right, the people have a corresponding duty; and for every privilege they enjoy, there is a trust for them to discharge. The large personal freedom possessed by the American citizens imposes equally as large public responsibilities. It is the duty of every citizen to obey the law, to aid in securing justice, to respect authority, to love his country, and to labor for the public good. No one can be a useful member of society unless he respects the laws and institutions of the land. The people themselves have established this government, both State and national; it exists for them, and therefore they owe it honor and obedience.

It is the duty of every voter to study the interests of the country, and to vote for persons and measures that, in his opinion, will best "promote the general welfare." In this country, government is intrusted to the whole people, and they can govern only by expressing their will in elections. Therefore the majority must rule. The majority will sometimes make mistakes, but these will be corrected after a time. In order that good government may ensue, good citizens must take part in elections. The privilege of suffrage is conferred upon an implied contract that it will be used for the public good. He who fails to vote when he can, fails to perform his part of the contract, fails to fulfill his promise, and fails to respect the government that protects him.

## CONSTITUTION.

The constitution is often called the supreme law of the State. In other words, it is the supreme act of the people, for the purpose of organizing themselves as a body politic, of formulating their government, and of fixing the limits of its power. It is a contract between the whole society as a political body, and each of its members. Each binds himself to the whole body, and the whole body binds itself to each, in order that all may be governed by the same laws for the common good. The constitution of each State is a written instrument, modeled after the Constitution of the United States, with which it must not conflict.

The constitutions of England and most other countries of Europe are unwritten. They consist of the common usages and maxims that have become fixed by long experience. In those countries, when a new political custom grows into common practice it thereby becomes a part of the national constitution.

FORMATION AND ADOPTION.--As the whole people can not assemble in one place to frame and adopt a constitution, they elect delegates to a constitutional convention. The convention usually meets at the capital, deliberates, frames articles for a proposed constitution, and in nearly all cases submits them to the people. The people make known their will in a general election, and if a majority vote in favor of adopting the proposed constitution, it becomes the constitution of the State. If the proposed constitution is rejected, another convention must be called to propose other articles to be voted upon by the people.

PURPOSES.--The purposes of the constitution are to guard the rights of the people, to protect the liberties of the minority, to grant authority to the government, to separate the functions of the three departments, to prescribe the limits of each, and to fix in the public policy those maxims of political wisdom that have been sanctioned by time.

The special tendency in recent amendments of State constitutions has been to limit the power of the legislature. Constitutions, like other political institutions, are largely matters of growth, and from time to time must be revised to meet the changing wants of society. For this purpose the constitution of almost every State contains a provision, called the open clause, which authorizes the legislature, under certain restrictions, to propose amendments to the constitution to be adopted or rejected by a vote of the people.

VALUE.--The people of any State may, at their pleasure, frame and adopt a new constitution, which must be in harmony with the Constitution of the United States. The right to make their own constitution is one of the highest and most important rights that freemen can possess. It is in this and in the right of suffrage that their freedom principally consists.

The constitution protects the people by prescribing the limits of official authority. The legislature can not legally pass a law which the constitution of the State forbids, and when such a law is passed it is declared unconstitutional by the State courts. A provision of a State constitution becomes void when declared by the supreme court of the United States to be in conflict with the national Constitution.

CONTENTS.--The constitutions of the several States are based upon the Constitution of the United States as a model, and are therefore much alike in their general provisions. Each contains:

A preamble setting forth the purposes of the constitution;

A lengthy declaration called the bill of rights;

Provisions for distributing the powers of government into three departments; and

Articles relating to suffrage, debt, taxation, corporations, public schools, militia, amendments, and other public affairs.

BILL OF RIGHTS.

The bill of rights usually declares various rights of the citizen which may be classified under the heads of republican principles, personal security, private property, freedom of conscience, freedom of speech and of the press, freedom of assembly, and freedom from military tyranny.

REPUBLICAN PRINCIPLES.--Under this head the bill declares:

That all power is inherent in the people;

That governments exist for their good, and by their consent;

That all freemen are equal;

That no title of nobility shall be conferred;

That exclusive privileges shall not be granted except in consideration of public services;

That all elections shall be free and equal.

PERSONAL SECURITY.--In the interests of the personal security of the citizen it is provided:

That the people shall be secure in their persons, houses, papers, and possessions, from unreasonable seizures and searches;

That warrants to seize and to search persons and things must describe them by oath or affirmation;

That there shall be no imprisonment for debt, except in cases of fraud.

PRIVATE PROPERTY.--To secure the rights of private property, the bill declares:

That private property shall not be taken for public use without just compensation;

And, in some States, that long leases of agricultural lands shall not be made.

FREEDOM OF CONSCIENCE.--To induce the entire freedom of conscience of the citizen it is declared:

That there shall be perfect religious freedom, but not covering immoral practices;

That there shall be no State church;

That no religious test shall be required for performing any public function;

That the rights of conscience are free from human control.

FREEDOM OF SPEECH AND OF THE PRESS.--To maintain the rightful freedom of the press, the bill guarantees:

That printing-presses may be used by all;

That every citizen may freely speak, write, and print upon any subject--being responsible for the abuse of the right.

FREEDOM OF ASSEMBLY.--The right of assembly is secured by the provision:

That the people may peaceably assemble for the public good, to discuss questions of public interest; and

That they may petition the government for redress of grievances.

FREEDOM FROM MILITARY TYRANNY.--To guard against abuses by the military, it is declared:

That the military shall be in strict subordination to the civil power;

That no standing army shall be maintained in time of peace;

That in time of peace no soldier shall be quartered in any house without the owner's consent;

That the right of people to bear arms shall not be questioned. This does not authorize the carrying of concealed weapons.

FORBIDDEN LAWS.--To insure the people against improper legislation, the bill of rights provides:

That no ex post facto law or law impairing the validity of contracts, shall be made;

That no bill of attainder shall be passed;

That no power of suspending laws shall be exercised except by the legislature.

RIGHTS OF THE ACCUSED.--Among the worst abuses of tyranny in all ages have been the corruption of the courts and the denial of the rights of common justice. To guard against these it is expressly provided:

That the writ of habeas corpus shall not be suspended except when, in cases of rebellion or invasion, the public safety may require it;

That, except in capital cases, persons charged with crime may give bail;

That no excessive bail shall be required;

That all courts shall be open;

That the accused shall have a speedy trial in the district in which the offense was committed;

That the ancient mode of trial by jury shall be maintained; but civil suits, by consent of the parties, may be tried without a jury;

That all persons injured in lands, goods, person, or reputation shall have remedy by course of law;

That the accused shall be informed of the nature of the charges against him;

That he shall be confronted by the witnesses against him;

That he shall be heard in his own defense, and may have the benefit of counsel;

That he shall not be required to testify against himself;

That he shall not be deprived of life, liberty, or property except by due process of law;

That no cruel or unusual punishment shall be inflicted;

That no one shall be twice placed in jeopardy for the same offense.

No citizen of the United States would deny the justice of these declarations. They are so reasonable it seems strange that they should ever have been questioned. "But in enumerating them we are treading on sacred ground. Their establishment cost our ancestors hundreds of years of struggle against arbitrary power, in which they gave their blood and treasure."[2]

It was to secure and maintain a part of these rights that the American colonies went to war with Great Britain, and made good their Declaration of Independence by an appeal to arms.

Most of these rights are preserved in the Constitution of the United States, to prevent encroachments upon the liberties of the people by the General Government. They are repeated in the State constitution in order that they may not be invaded by the State Government. There is also a provision in the constitution of the State which declares that "the enumeration of certain rights shall not be construed to deny or disparage others retained by the people."

[1]Popular education must command the sympathy and respect of the people in each locality in order to remain "popular." While the State, therefore, enforces a general system of public schools, it leaves all the details of local

management with the people most closely related to the particular school. The people esteem that which they create and control.

[2]McCleary's Studies in Civics.

SUGGESTIVE QUESTIONS.

1. Why are the smaller political communities subject to the State?

2. Give the names of the thirteen original States.

3. What is meant by States having different industries and occupations?

4. How do State institutions develop the self-reliance of the people?

5. Name some acts of government which you have seen the State perform.

6. What are charitable institutions?

7. How is justice administered?

8. Wherein are the people of this country freer than other people?

9. How long must a person live in this State to entitle him to vote?

10. What is meant by being secure in person?

11. Read the bill of rights in the constitution of your State.

12. What is a body politic?

13. Why can not the whole people assemble to form a State constitution?

14. What is meant by taking private property for public use?

15. How may the right to speak and print be abused?

16. What is meant by the military being subordinate to the civil power?

17. Are all cases tried by jury?

QUESTION FOR DEBATE.

Resolved, That there should be an educational qualification for suffrage.

CHAPTER VIII.

THE STATE--(Continued).

GOVERNMENT DEPARTMENTS.--The State government is based upon the State constitution. It has a legislative department charged with the making of the laws, an executive department to enforce the laws, and a judicial department to explain and apply the laws. Each of the departments is independent of the others, being supreme within its own sphere.

The American people believe that the functions of making, of enforcing, and of explaining the laws, should forever be separate and distinct. Experience has shown that it is dangerous to the liberties of the people to permit either of the three departments of government to trespass upon the functions of the others. Therefore, the limits of each department are well defined, and its power closely guarded, by the constitution and laws of the State.

LEGISLATIVE DEPARTMENT.

The legislative or law-making power of the State is vested in the legislature, sometimes called the general assembly, and in some States known as the general court, or legislative assembly. The legislature is composed of two bodies, or houses, called respectively the Senate and the House of Representatives. In New York the latter body is known as the Assembly, in New Jersey it is called the General Assembly and in some States the House of Delegates. A bill must be passed by both branches of the legislature in order to become a law. The proceedings of the legislature should be made public, and therefore the sessions are open, and the constitution requires each house to keep and publish a daily record, called the Journal.

QUALIFICATIONS.--The State constitution prescribes the age, the length of residence, and other legal qualifications for membership in each branch of the legislature. The constitutions of most States fix a longer term of office and require a more mature age for senators than for representatives. In addition to these legal qualifications a legislator should be a man of unswerving honesty, of broad information, of close thought, well versed in the principles of government, acquainted with the needs of the country, and faithful to the interests of the whole people.

PRIVILEGES.--Each branch of the legislature consists of members elected by the people. Senators and representatives are responsible for their official acts to the people, and to the people alone. Except for treason, felony, and breach of the peace, members of the legislature are privileged from arrest while attending the sessions of their respective houses, and while going thereto and returning therefrom. For any speech or debate in either house, a member thereof can not be questioned in any other place.

Each house adopts rules for its own government. Each house also elects its own officers, except that in most States the people elect a lieutenant-governor, who is also president of the Senate. These various privileges are granted in the State constitution in order that the actions of the legislature may be free from all outside influences.

POWER.--The constitution of the State defines the limits of the power vested in the legislative department. The legislature may enact any law not forbidden by the Constitution of the State or of the United States. Every act passed is binding upon the people unless it is declared by the courts to be unconstitutional. An act of the legislature, when declared to be unconstitutional, thereby becomes void; that is, it ceases to have any legal force.

SESSIONS.--The legislature meets at the State Capitol. In a few States the legislature holds annual sessions, but in far the greater number it meets biennially; that is, once every two years. In many States the constitution limits the session to a certain number of days, but in a few of these States the legislature may extend its session by a special vote of two-thirds of each house. A majority constitutes a quorum for business, but a smaller number may meet and adjourn from day to day in order that the organization may not be lost.

FUNCTIONS.--The legislature enacts laws upon a great variety of subjects. It fixes the rate of State taxation, it provides for the collection and distribution of State revenue, creates offices and fixes salaries, provides for a system of popular education, and makes laws relating to public works, the administration of justice, the conduct of elections, the management of railways and other corporations, the maintenance of charitable and other institutions, the construction and repair of public roads, the organization of the militia, the conduct of prisons and reformatories, and a number of other public interests.

FORBIDDEN POWERS.--The Constitution of the United States forbids any State to exercise certain powers:

(1) No State can enter into any treaty, alliance, confederation, contract, or agreement with any other State, or with a foreign power; issue commissions to vessels authorizing them to capture and destroy the merchant ships of other nations; coin money; issue paper money; make any thing but gold and silver coin a legal tender for the payment of debts; pass any bill inflicting the penalty of death without a regular trial, or any law fixing a penalty for acts done before its adoption, or any law affecting the provisions of contracts made before its passage; or grant any title of nobility.

(2) No State can, without the consent of Congress, lay a tax or duty on imports or exports, except what is necessary in executing its inspection laws. The net proceeds of all duties laid by any State for this purpose must be paid into the treasury of the United States; and all such laws are subject to the revision and control of Congress. Without the consent of Congress, no State can tax ships, keep troops or ships of war in time of peace, or engage in war unless invaded or in imminent danger.

(3) "No State shall make or enforce any law which shall abridge the privileges or immunities of citizens of the United States; nor shall any State deprive any person of life, liberty, or property without due process of law, nor deny to any person within its jurisdiction the equal protection of the laws."

(4) "[No] State shall assume or pay any debt or obligation incurred in aid of insurrection or rebellion against the United States, or any claim for loss or emancipation of any slave."

THE SENATE.--The Senate is a less numerous body than the House of Representatives. The presiding officer is addressed as "Mr. President" or "Mr. Speaker," the title varying in different States. There is also a chief clerk, with assistants, who keeps the records; a sergeant-at-arms, who preserves order on the floor; a doorkeeper, who has charge of the senate chamber and its entrances, and a number of subordinate officers.

The Senate has two functions not belonging to the House of Representatives: 1. When the governor nominates persons for appointment as officers of the State, unless the Senate advises and consents to the nominations, the appointments are void; 2. When the House of Representatives presents articles of impeachment against an officer of the State, the Senate sits as a court to try the charges.

HOUSE OF REPRESENTATIVES.--The House of Representatives is often called the popular branch of the legislature. It is sometimes designated as the "House." The title of the presiding officer is "Mr. Speaker." The other officers usually have the same titles and duties as those of the Senate.

In many States bills raising revenue, and in some States bills making appropriations, must originate in the House of Representatives. This body also has the sole power of impeachment. Usually when charges affecting the official conduct of an officer of the State are brought before the legislature, the House of Representatives appoints a committee to investigate the charges and report. If the report warrants further action, the House adopts charges of official misconduct, or of high crimes and misdemeanors in office. This proceeding is called an impeachment.

The Senate sits as a court of impeachment, hears the evidence, listens to the argument by the managers and the counsel for the accused, and then condemns or acquits. The judgment in cases of impeachment is removal from office and disqualification to hold any office of honor, trust, or profit under the State.

DIRECT LEGISLATION.--In order to give fuller and quicker effect to the will of the people in law making, recent provisions in the constitutions of some States provide for the initiative and referendum. By the initiative a certain number of voters may petition for the enactment of a law set forth in the petition. If the legislature does not pass the act petitioned for, it may be enacted by the people, voting on it in a general or special election--the referendum. On petition of a certain number of voters also, a referendum may be ordered as to a bill passed by the legislature, to which the petitioners object, giving the people the opportunity to ratify or reject the proposed law.

These methods of direct legislation have been applied also to the making of constitutional amendments, and to some city, as well as some state governments.

## SUGGESTIVE QUESTIONS.

1. Why is the State legislature composed of two houses?

2. Why should the proceedings of the legislature be public?

3. Why should senators and representatives be free from arrest while discharging their public duties?

4. How often does the legislature of this State meet?

5. What is the limit of its session?

6. Can its session be extended?

7. What is a reformatory?

8. What are the age and number of years of residence required of a State senator in this State? Who is the senator from this district?

9. What is a bill for raising revenue?

10. What are the age and number of years of residence required of a representative in this State? Who is the representative from this district?

## QUESTION FOR DEBATE

Resolved, That a State legislature should not have more than forty senators and one hundred representatives.

# CHAPTER IX.

## THE STATE--(Continued).

When the laws are enacted it becomes necessary that some one be charged with seeing that they are duly executed and obeyed. The people's representatives in the legislative department make the laws. The people's servants in the executive department execute the laws.

## EXECUTIVE DEPARTMENT.

The chief executive officers of the State are the governor, the lieutenant-governor, the secretary of state, the auditor or comptroller, the treasurer, the attorney-general, and the superintendent of public instruction, who, in most States, are elected by the people. Besides these, an adjutant-general, a commissioner of agriculture, a commissioner of insurance, railway commissioners, a register of the land office or land commissioner, and in some States other subordinate officers, are usually appointed by the governor, and confirmed by the Senate.

The higher State offices are provided for in the constitution, while the subordinate offices are created by act of the legislature. Several States have no lieutenant-governor; in some the secretary of state and the superintendent of public instruction are appointed by the governor, and in others some of the subordinate officers are elected by the people. The titles of many of these officers vary in different States.

The terms of the State officers elected by the people are usually alike in the same State, but in some States there are differences. In several States the terms of the auditor and the treasurer are less than those of the other officers.

GOVERNOR: TERM, QUALIFICATIONS.--The supreme executive authority is vested in the governor, who is therefore sometimes called the chief executive of the State. His position is one of great dignity and influence.

The term of office is one, two, three, or four years, varying in different States, and in some the constitution prohibits any person from serving two terms in succession.

The legal qualifications of the office of governor vary in different States. He must be a citizen of the United States; must have resided in the State at least a fixed term of years; must not be under a certain age, usually thirty years; and in some States must own property of a given value.

POWERS, DUTIES.--The governor is commander-in-chief of the military forces of the State, and represents it in its dealings with other States. He may call on all other executive officers for written information concerning their respective duties. He is presumed to be well informed upon the affairs of the people, and is therefore required to give the legislature information as to the condition of the State, and to recommend the passage of such laws as he deems proper and expedient.

The governor may call special meetings of the legislature to consider questions of great and immediate public concern. At the opening of each session he addresses a regular message to the legislature, and from time to time submits special messages upon various subjects.

All acts of the legislature are presented for his approval and signature. If he approves and signs them, they become laws; if he retains them for a certain number of days without signing them, they become laws without his signature; if he refuses to approve them, he returns them within the specified time to the house in which they originated, with a statement of his objections.

This action is called a veto, and the vetoed measure, in order to become a law, must pass both houses again, and in some States must secure a two thirds vote of each house.

The governor may grant reprieves and pardons, except in cases of impeachment, and in some States, of treason. In some States this power is limited by a board of pardons, which must recommend a pardon before it can be granted by the governor; and in others the consent of one branch of the legislature must be obtained.

Treason against the States consists in an open or overt act of "levying war against them, or in adhering to their enemies, giving them aid and comfort."

To reprieve is to delay or postpone for a time the execution of the sentence of death upon a criminal.

To pardon is to annul a sentence by forgiving the offense against the law, and by releasing the offender.

The governor may also commute the sentence of an offender by exchanging the penalty for one less severe.

LIEUTENANT-GOVERNOR:--The term and qualifications of the lieutenant-governor are the same as those of the governor. The lieutenant-governor is also president or speaker of the Senate, but votes only in case of a tie. In States having no lieutenant-governor, the Senate elects its presiding officer.

In case of the death or resignation of the governor, the lieutenant-governor becomes governor of the State. In States having no lieutenant-governor, special laws provide for filling vacancies in the office of governor.

When the chief executive is absent from the State, or disabled, the lieutenant-governor performs the duties of the office.

SECRETARY OF STATE.--The secretary of state is the keeper of all State papers, and usually of the great seal of the State. In some States he is ex officio auditor. He keeps a record of the proceedings and acts of the legislature and of the executive department of the State government.

He certifies to the correctness of State documents and commissions, indexes the laws, and attends to their printing and distribution, except in States having a superintendent of printing. He receives and preserves the returns of elections, and in some States has charge of the State buildings at the capital.

AUDITOR, OR COMPTROLLER.--The auditor is the financial agent of the State, and in some States acts as register of the land office, and in others as commissioner of insurance. He is also the State's bookkeeper, and attends to the collection of its revenue. He examines and adjusts claims and accounts against the State, and orders the payment of such as he approves. He receives moneys paid to the State, deposits them with the treasurer, and takes receipt therefor. No funds can be paid out of the State treasury except upon the auditor's warrant. He makes an annual or biennial report, showing the financial condition of the State. In some States having no auditor, these various duties fall to other officers, chiefly to the secretary of state.

TREASURER.--The treasurer is custodian of the funds of the State. He receives the State's revenues from the auditor, and pays them out only upon the auditor's warrant, keeping an accurate account of all sums paid. The treasurer and the auditor (and also the secretary of state when he handles State funds) give heavy bonds for the faithful performance of their duties.

ATTORNEY-GENERAL.--The attorney-general is a lawyer who acts as attorney for the State in law cases to which the State is a party. His duties pertain chiefly to the higher courts of the State. He is the legal adviser of the State officers, and, when requested by them, gives opinions upon points of law.

He prosecutes persons who are indebted to the State, and assists in bringing to justice those charged with crime. He represents the State in its legal business in the supreme court at Washington, and in the other courts of the United States.

SUPERINTENDENT OF PUBLIC INSTRUCTION.--The superintendent of public instruction has charge of the public school system, and thus superintends one of the largest interests of the State. He has the general management of State teachers' institutes, and in some States he has an official connection with the State university and the State normal schools, either as a member of the faculty or as president or secretary of the board of trustees.

He is an officer of, and usually president of, the State board of education, a body generally consisting of from three to seven members, and in most States composed, in part, of other high officers of the State. The State board of education decides questions of school law, and performs other important duties varying in different States.

The superintendent of public instruction makes an annual or biennial report to the legislature, showing the condition of the public schools and suggesting amendments to the system. In many States the superintendent is elected by the people; in some he is appointed by the governor; in others he is elected by the State board of education, and, as president or secretary of that board, is ex efficio superintendent of public instruction.

OTHER OFFICERS.--The adjutant-general is the active officer of the State militia.

The commissioner of agriculture, sometimes called the secretary of the board of agriculture, looks after the agricultural interests of the State.

The commissioner of insurance oversees the insurance companies doing business in the State.

The railway commissioners assess the value of railway property, and to a limited extent regulate charges on railway lines.

The register of the land office, or land commissioner, keeps in his office the patents or title-deeds of land issued by the State in its early settlement, and furnishes copies of land patents and warrants to those who desire them. In a few States this officer is elected by the people.

The State librarian has charge of the State library, and in some States is superintendent of the State buildings at the capital.

In a few States there are other executive officers, among whom may be named:

A surveyor-general, who surveys the public lands, and keeps in his office maps of counties and townships;

A State engineer, who superintends the construction and repair of canals and levees;

A commissioner of statistics, who collects statistics relating to public interests;

A commissioner of immigration, who attends to the interests of immigrants;

A labor commissioner, who looks after the interests of the laboring classes;

A bank inspector, or superintendent of banking, who inspects State banks for the protection of the public; and

A State examiner, who investigates the conduct of State institutions, and inspects the State offices, in order to secure honesty and efficiency in public affairs.

In some States two or more of these offices are combined, and in others their duties are performed by the higher officers of the State.

SUGGESTIVE QUESTIONS.

1. What is the term of office and what the name of the governor of this State?

2. What are the age and the length of residence required of him?

3. How many terms can he serve in succession?

4. Has this State a lieutenant-governor?

5. If so, name his qualifications.

6. What is the great seal of the State?

7. What is the necessity of an auditor?

8. Why should the superintendent of public instruction make a report?

QUESTION FOR DEBATE

Resolved, That the governor should hold the power of veto.

CHAPTER X.

THE STATE--(Continued).

## JUDICIAL DEPARTMENT.

PURPOSES.--The judicial department of the State government exists for the sole purpose of administering justice; that is, for the purpose of interpreting the laws and of applying them to particular cases. The legislature makes the laws, but it can not execute them. The governor recommends the passage of certain laws, and holds the veto power; but he has no law-making power, nor can he try the most trivial suit.

So the judiciary has no voice in making or in executing the laws, its sole function being to decide their meaning and to apply them in securing justice. The legislative and executive departments may assist, but it is the peculiar province of the judiciary to protect society and to maintain the rights of the people.

SUPREME COURT.--The higher courts of the State are of two classes--those whose jurisdiction includes the entire State, and those whose jurisdiction is confined to particular districts.

The Supreme Court, called in some States the Court of Appeals, is the highest court of the State. The number of the judges of the supreme court varies in the different States, there being a chief justice and from two to eight associate justices in each State.

In some States the Justices are elected by the people; in others they are elected by the legislature; and in some they are appointed by the governor, and confirmed by the Senate.

The term of office is lengthy, not less than four years in any State, except Vermont, where it is two years; six, seven, eight, nine, ten, twelve, fourteen, or fifteen years in most States; twenty-one years in Pennsylvania; during good behavior in Massachusetts; until the judges are seventy years of age in New Hampshire; and practically for life in Rhode Island.

The jurisdiction of the supreme court, or court of appeals, extends over the entire State. It holds sessions at the State capital, and in some States at other prominent places, and is chiefly engaged in the trial of cases in which appeals have been taken from the decisions of the lower courts.

Its decision is final, but in cases in which it is alleged that the State law is in conflict with the constitution or laws of the United States, appeals may be taken to the United States Supreme Court at Washington.

DISTRICT, OR CIRCUIT COURT.--The people most commonly resort to the district court, circuit court, or superior court, as it is variously called in different States, to secure justice. In it are tried the great body of important civil and criminal cases, and also appeals from the lower courts.

The jurisdiction of the district court is limited to a district created by the State constitution or by act of the State legislature. In some cases the district consists of a single county; usually it includes two or more counties, the court being held successively in each county of the district.

In each district there is usually one district judge, who is elected by the people, appointed by the governor, or elected by the legislature.

The term of office in most States is four, six, or eight years.

In some of the districts of certain States there are criminal courts having jurisdiction in criminal cases, and chancery courts or courts of common pleas having jurisdiction in certain civil cases.

In some States there is a high court of chancery having State jurisdiction, and in others there is a superior court which has State jurisdiction, and whose rank is between the supreme court and the district courts.

TERRITORIES.

ORGANIZATION.--Congress organizes the public domain into Territories, fixes their boundaries, and establishes their governments. The act of organization is passed as soon as the population is dense enough to require governmental authority.

EXECUTIVE DEPARTMENT.--The governor and the secretary of the Territory are appointed by the President of the United States, with the consent of the United States Senate, and serve for four years, unless removed. The governor appoints a treasurer, an auditor or comptroller, a superintendent of public instruction, an attorney-general, and several other territorial officers.

LEGISLATIVE DEPARTMENT.--The legislature consists of a senate of eight or fifteen members, and a house of representatives of sixteen or thirty members elected by the people of the Territory. The senate is sometimes called the upper house of the legislature. Although the governor and the legislature rule the Territory, all laws passed by them must be submitted to Congress, and, if disapproved, they become null and void.

JUDICIAL DEPARTMENT.--The judiciary consists of a supreme court and inferior courts. The chief justice and two or more associate justices of the supreme court are appointed for four years by the President, with the consent of the Senate. The inferior courts are established by the territorial legislature.

REPRESENTATION IN CONGRESS.--Each Territory elects a delegate to the Congress of the United States. Territorial delegates serve upon committees, and have the right to debate, but not to vote. Their real duties are as agents of their respective Territories.

LAWS.--Territories are governed by the laws of Congress, by the common law, and by the laws passed by the territorial legislatures. The governor may pardon offenses against territorial laws, and may grant reprieves for offenses against the laws of Congress, until the cases can be acted upon by the President.

LOCAL AFFAIRS.--The local interests of a Territory are similar to those of a State. Taxation, schools, public works, and the administration of justice are supported by the people. The people of the Territories have no voice in the election of President, and none in the government of the United States except through their delegates in Congress.

PURPOSES.--The chief purposes of the territorial government are to give the people the protection of the law, and to prepare the Territory for admission into the Union as a State. A State is a member of the Union, with all the rights and privileges of self-government; a Territory is under the Union, subject at all times, and in all things, to regulation by the government of the United States.

All the States, except the original thirteen (including Maine, Vermont, Kentucky, and West Virginia) and California and Texas, have had territorial governments. A Territory is not entirely self-governing; it may be called a State in infancy, requiring the special care of the United States to prepare it for statehood and for admission into the Union "upon an equal footing with the original States in all respects."

Hawaii and Alaska illustrate the territorial form of government described above. The following are exceptions to the rule:

The District of Columbia is neither a State nor a Territory. It resembles a Territory in being directly governed by Congress in such manner as that body may choose, but it differs from a Territory since it can never become a State.

It is not represented in the government of the United States, and its inhabitants have no voice in local matters. Its affairs are administered by three commissioners, appointed by the President, with the consent of the Senate, and they are subject to the laws of Congress.

Porto Rico and Philippines have each a legislature and are governed much like a Territory; but their people are not citizens of the United States. They are practically colonies.

SUGGESTIVE QUESTIONS.

1. Is it better that judges be elected, or that they be appointed? Why?

2. Why should a judge's term of office be lengthy?

3. Who is chief justice of this State?

4. Who is the judge of the circuit or district court of this district?

5. At what dates does this court hold sessions in this county?

6. How many organized Territories now in the United States? Give their names.

7. When did this State cease to be a Territory?

8. Why should delegates from the Territories not have the privilege of voting in Congress?

QUESTION FOR DEBATE.

Resolved, That the judges of the higher courts should be appointed by the governor, and hold their positions during life and good behavior.

CHAPTER XI.

THE UNITED STATES.

INTRODUCTORY.--Each division of government which we have considered exists for only a part of the whole people. The government of one State has no authority over the people of other States; but the government of the United States, often called the national government or federal government, is for the good of the entire country, and its authority is over the whole people.

All these divisions of government--the family, the school, the township or civil district, the county, the State, and the United States--are dependent upon one another.

If family government were destroyed, society would be ruined and other governments would be worthless.

If there were no schools, the people would be so ignorant that free government would be impossible.

If the township or civil district were neglected, local government would be inefficient.

If the States were blotted out, the national government would assume all power, and the freedom of the people would be greatly abridged, and perhaps finally lost.

If the national government were dismembered, the States would be weak, helpless, at war with one another, and at the mercy of foreign nations.

The distribution of power among the several political organizations prevents any of them from assuming too much authority, and thus tends to preserve the liberties of the people.

FORMATION.--The national government is based upon the Constitution of the United States. It was formed by the union of the several States under the Constitution, and its powers are set forth in that instrument. The thirteen original States ratified the Constitution of the United States between December 7, 1787, and May 29, 1790, and thus organized the national government. It thus became, and has continued to be, the government of the whole people, "by the people and for the people."

FORM OF GOVERNMENT.

The national government, like the government of each State, is a republic; that is, the authority is exercised by the representatives of the people. As all power resides in the people, our government is called a democracy. As the people elect officers or representatives to act for them in the performance of public duties, it is called a representative democracy.

Our system of government is different from those of all other nations, because part of the political power is vested in the State, and part in the nation; that is, in the United States.

The national Constitution enumerates the powers which may be exercised by the national government, and reserves all other powers "to the States respectively, or to the people." Because of this dual or double character of our system of government, John Quincy Adams called it "a complicated machine."

PURPOSES.--The purposes of the national government are clearly and forcibly set forth in the "preamble," or opening clause, of the Constitution of the United States;

1. "To form a more perfect union;"

2. "To establish justice;"

3. "To insure domestic tranquillity;"

4. "To provide for the common defense;"

5. "To promote the general welfare;"

6. "To secure the blessings of liberty to ourselves and our posterity."

Before the Revolutionary war, the American colonies were subject to Great Britain. By the Declaration of Independence these colonies became "free and independent States." During the period between the Declaration of Independence and the adoption of the national Constitution, the union between the States was weak and unsatisfactory.

Instead of there being "domestic tranquillity," the States were engaged in constant quarrels. There was no power to provide for the "common defense" of the people against foreign enemies; each State must protect itself as best it could. No provision could be made for the "general welfare" by the passage and enforcement of broad measures for the whole country. Under the Articles of Confederation, as was said at that time, the States might "declare everything, but do nothing." The adoption of the national Constitution and the formation of the national government made the inhabitants of the States one people, and have since brought the United States to be "the first of the nations of the earth."

FUNCTIONS.--The functions of the national government are numerous and important. In adopting the national Constitution, the States delegated or ceded to the United States those powers which are necessary to the strength and greatness of a nation.

The national government administers those public affairs which concern the whole people, such as the regulation of commerce, the granting of patents, and the coinage of money; and also those which pertain to the United States as a nation dealing with other nations, such as declaring war and making treaties of peace.

The subjects upon which the national Congress may enact laws, and consequently the subjects included in the functions of the national government, are enumerated in Section 8, Article I. of the Constitution.

CITIZENS.

The people who reside in the United States are either citizens or aliens. The national Constitution declares that "All persons born or naturalized in the United States, and subject to the jurisdiction thereof, are citizens of the United States and of the State wherein they reside." Women and children are citizens, though not entitled to vote.

A citizen is a member of the body politic, bound to allegiance, and entitled to protection at home and abroad. He can renounce his allegiance--that is, lay down his citizenship--by becoming the subject of some other country. Wherever he goes, until he renounces his allegiance, he is a citizen of the United States, and is shielded from insult by the might and majesty of the whole nation. Citizenship is therefore valuable for its protection abroad, as well as for its rights and privileges at home.

NATURALIZATION.--Naturalized citizens are persons of foreign birth who have become citizens by naturalization, after a continuous residence of at least five years in the United States. A foreigner is naturalized by appearing in court, declaring his intention to become a citizen of the United States, and his purpose to renounce all allegiance to foreign governments. After two years more, he must appear in open court, renounce upon oath all foreign allegiance, and swear to support the Constitution of the United States. If he bears any title of nobility, he must renounce it. Naturalized citizens have all the rights and privileges that belong to native-born citizens, except that no naturalized person can become President or Vice President of the United States.

RIGHTS.--The Constitution of the United States does not contain a formal bill of rights, as do most of the State constitutions, but it names the following as among the rights of citizens:

(1) "The citizens of each State shall be entitled to all privileges and immunities of citizens of the several States";

That is, a citizen who removes into another State shall enjoy all the rights and privileges that belong to its citizens.

(2) "A person charged in any State with treason, felony, or other crime, who shall flee from justice, and be found in another State, shall, on demand of the executive authority of the State from which he fled, be delivered up, to be removed to the State having jurisdiction of the crime." A demand for the delivery of a fugitive criminal is called a requisition.

(3) "No person held to service or labor in one State under the laws thereof, escaping into another, shall, in consequence of any law or regulation therein, be discharged from such service or labor; but shall be delivered up on claim of the party to whom such service or labor may be due."

This provision refers to the capture and return of fugitive slaves, and is rendered void by the abolition of slavery.

(4) "A well-regulated militia being necessary to the security of a free State, the right of the people to keep and bear arms shall not be infringed."

This clause does not authorize the carrying of concealed weapons.

(5) "No soldier shall, in time of peace, be quartered in any house without the consent of the owner, nor in time of war but in a manner to be prescribed by law."

(6) "The right of the people to be secure in their persons, houses, papers, and effects, against unreasonable searches and seizures, shall not be violated; and no warrants shall issue but upon probable cause, supported by oath or affirmation, and particularly describing the place to be searched and the persons or things to be seized."

(7) a. "No person shall be held to answer for a capital or otherwise infamous crime, unless on a presentment or indictment of a grand jury, except in cases arising in the land or naval forces, or in the militia when in actual service, in time of war or public danger;

b. "Nor shall any person be subject for the same offense to be twice put in jeopardy of life or limb, nor shall be compelled, in any criminal case, to be a witness against himself;

c. "Nor be deprived of life, liberty, or property without due process of law;

d. "Nor shall private property be taken for public use without just compensation."

The first part of this clause secures a civil trial to every private citizen. The land and naval forces, and the militia when in actual service, are under military law, usually called martial law.

(8) "In all criminal prosecutions the accused shall enjoy the right

a. "To a speedy and public trial by an impartial jury of the State and district wherein the crime shall have been committed, which district shall have been previously ascertained by law;

b. "To be informed of the nature and cause of the accusation;

c. "To be confronted with the witnesses against him;

d. "To have compulsory process for obtaining witnesses in his favor;

e. "And to have the assistance of counsel for his defense."

(9) "In suits at law where the value in controversy shall exceed twenty dollars, the right of trial by jury shall be preserved, and no fact tried by a jury shall be otherwise re-examined in any court of the United States than according to the rules of the common law."

(10) "Excessive bail shall not be required, nor excessive fines imposed, nor cruel and unusual punishment inflicted."

(11) "Neither slavery nor involuntary servitude, except as a punishment for crime whereof the party shall have been duly convicted, shall exist within the United States or any place subject to their jurisdiction."

(12) "The right of citizens of the United States to vote shall not be denied or

abridged by the United States, or by any State, on account of race, color, or previous condition of servitude."

(13) "The enumeration in the Constitution of certain rights shall not be construed to deny or disparage others retained by the people."

ALIENS.

Aliens are subjects of foreign governments. They are not citizens of this country, and, in general, have no right to take part in its political affairs. Throughout the Union aliens have full social and moral rights; in some States their property rights are restricted; and in a few States they have certain political rights.

NATURE OF THE CONSTITUTION.

The Constitution of the United States is the supreme law of the whole land. It is a written instrument, and is often called the fundamental law.

Neither the laws of any State nor the laws of the United States must conflict with the Constitution. It is the basis of our system of government, the model upon which all State constitutions are framed, and the foundation of our greatness as a people. It defines the limits of the national government, and enumerates the powers of each of its departments. It declares what public interests are within the scope of the national government, reserves certain powers to the States, and provides that neither State nor nation shall enact certain specified laws.

FORMATION.--The national Constitution was framed by a convention of delegates from twelve of the thirteen original States, Rhode Island alone being unrepresented. The convention was called for the purpose of revising the Articles of Confederation under which the States were at the time united.

The convention met at Philadelphia, on Monday, May 14, 1787, and organized on the 25th day of the same month by electing as its president George Washington, one of the delegates from Virginia. The Articles of Confederation were readily seen to be inadequate to the purposes of a national government, and the convention proceeded to draught a "Constitution for the

United States of America."

The convention completed its labors, submitted the Constitution to the several States for their ratification, and adjourned on the 17th of September, 1787. All the States ratified the Constitution, the last being Rhode Island, whose convention, called for the purpose, passed the ordinance of ratification, May 29, 1790.

NECESSITY.--The necessity for a written national constitution is readily seen. The preamble states the purposes of the Constitution, which are also the purposes of the national government. The Constitution defines the limits of State and of national power, and thus prevents conflicts of authority which would otherwise arise between the State and the United States. Through the Constitution, the people, who are the sources of all just authority, grant to the government certain powers, and reserve all other powers to themselves. The Constitution prescribes the functions of each department of the government, and thus preserves the liberties of the people by preventing either Congress, the executive department, or the judiciary from exercising powers not granted to it.

AMENDMENT.--The Constitution prescribes two methods by which it may be amended:

1. By a two thirds vote of both houses Congress may propose to the several States amendments to the Constitution.

2. Upon the application of two thirds of the States, Congress shall call a convention of delegates from the several States for proposing amendments.

An amendment proposed by either method, "when ratified by the legislatures of three fourths of the States, or by conventions in three fourths thereof, shall be valid to all intents and purposes as a part of this Constitution."

Twenty-one amendments have been proposed by Congress, and seventeen of these have been ratified by three fourths of the State legislatures, and have become parts of the Constitution. The other four proposed amendments were rejected. Congress has never called a convention to propose amendments, and no State has ever called a convention to consider those amendments proposed by Congress.

DEPARTMENTS.--The functions of each branch of government are carefully marked in the Constitution, and the people and their representatives jealously guard the rights of each department. They believe that the duties of the law-making power, those of the law-enforcing power, and those of the law-explaining power can not be too clearly separated. If the same officers could make the law, enforce the law, and explain the law, there would be no limit to their authority, and therefore no security to the people.

The framers of the Constitution were wise men; they had seen the abuse of power by Great Britain while the colonies were under her sway, and they determined to guard the liberties of the people by forever separating the legislative, the executive, and the judicial functions. Their example has been followed in the constitutions of all the States.

The President has no right to interfere with the decisions of the courts, and, except by his veto, can not interfere with the action of Congress.

Congress can not question the decisions of courts, nor can it interfere with the legal actions of the President, except that the Senate may refuse to confirm his appointments to office.

Even the Supreme Court of the United States can not call in question the official acts of the President, so long as he conforms to the law; nor has it any power over the acts of Congress, except merely to decide upon the constitutionality of the laws when they are properly brought before it.

While, therefore, Congress and the President have some remote influence upon the actions of each other, neither has the slightest right to invade the functions of the Supreme Court, or of any other court, even the humblest in the land.

SUGGESTIVE QUESTIONS.

1. Why do foreigners become naturalized?

2. What is a title of nobility?

3. What officer of a State makes requisition for the delivery of a criminal held by another State?

4. When was slavery abolished in the United States?

5. What is the purpose of a militia force?

6. What is a capital crime?

7. Why is the accused entitled to a speedy and public trial?

8. Why is the Constitution called the fundamental law?

9. Read in the history of the United States the account of the formation of the Constitution.

10. How many States were needed to ratify the Constitution in order that it might go into effect?

11. Read the amendments to the Constitution.

12. Can you name any proposed amendments that have been recently advocated?

QUESTION FOR DEBATE.

Resolved, That a written constitution is best for a free country.

CHAPTER XII.

THE UNITED STATES--(Continued).

LEGISLATIVE DEPARTMENT.

CONGRESS.--The legislative authority of the national government is vested in the Congress of the United States, consisting of a senate and a house of representatives. The senators represent the States, and the representatives represent the people. Congress holds annual sessions at the city of Washington, the seat of the national government. A measure must pass both houses, and be approved by the President, in order to become a law; or if vetoed, it fails, unless it again passes both houses by a two thirds vote.

Senators and representatives receive an annual salary of seven thousand five hundred dollars each; and are allowed mileage, or traveling expenses, of twenty cents for each mile in going to and returning from the session of Congress.

PRIVILEGES OF THE HOUSES.--There are certain constitutional privileges guaranteed to Congress in order that its action in legislation may be free from undue influence from other departments of the government.

"The times, places, and manner of holding elections for senators and representatives shall be prescribed in each State by the legislature thereof; but the Congress may, at any time, by law, make or alter such regulations, except as to the places of choosing senators.

"Each house shall be the judge of the elections, returns, and qualifications of its own members;" that is, each House declares who are entitled to membership therein.

"Each house may determine the rules of its proceedings, punish its members for disorderly conduct, and with the concurrence of two thirds expel a member."

Each house keeps and publishes a journal of its proceedings, "excepting such parts as may, in their judgment, require secrecy; and the yeas and nays of the members of either house, on any question, shall, at the desire of one fifth of those present, be entered on the journal."

"Neither house, during the session of Congress, shall, without the consent of the other, adjourn for more than three days, nor to any other place than that in which the two houses shall be sitting."

PRIVILEGES AND DISABILITIES OF MEMBERS.--The Constitution of the United States sets forth the following privileges and disabilities relating to membership in both the Senate and the House of Representatives:

(1) "The senators and representatives shall receive a compensation for their services, to be ascertained by law, and paid out of the treasury of the United States.

"They shall in all cases except treason, felony, and breach of the peace be privileged from arrest during their attendance at the session of their respective houses, and in going to and returning from the same; and for any speech or debate in either house they shall not be questioned in any other place."

(2) "No senator or representative shall, during the time for which he was elected, be appointed to any civil office under the authority of the United States which shall have been created, or the emoluments whereof shall have been increased, during such time; and no person holding any office under the United States shall be a member of either house during his continuance of office."

The purpose of the first part of this clause is to prevent members of Congress from voting to create offices, or to affix high salaries to offices, with the hope of being appointed to fill them.

(3) "The senators and representatives before mentioned, and the members of the several State legislatures, and all executive and judicial officers both of the United States and of the several States, shall be bound by oath or affirmation to support this Constitution; but no religious test shall ever be required as a qualification to any office or public trust under the United States."

(4) "No person shall be a senator or representative in Congress, or elector of President and Vice President, or hold any office, civil or military, under the United States, or under any State, who, having previously taken an oath as a member of Congress, or as an officer of the United States, or as a member of any State legislature, or as an executive or judicial officer of any State, to support the Constitution of the United States, shall have engaged in insurrection or rebellion against the same, or given aid and comfort to the enemies thereof. But Congress may, by a vote of two thirds of each House, remove such disability."

The purpose of the clause was to exclude from office all those who had sworn, as officers of the State or the nation, to support the Constitution of the United States, and who afterward engaged in war against the Union. An act of Congress enabling them to hold office was called a removal of their disabilities. This clause of the Constitution is practically void as regards all past offenses, as the disabilities of nearly all to whom it applied have been removed by Congress.

POWERS OF CONGRESS.--Congress has power:

(1) To levy and collect taxes, duties on imported goods, and revenues from articles of manufacture, "to pay the debts and provide for the common defense and general welfare of the United States."

(2) "To borrow money on the credit of the United States."

The usual method of borrowing money is to issue government bonds, which are promises to pay the sums specified in them at a given time, with interest at a given rate. The bonds are sold, usually at their face value, and the proceeds applied to public purposes. United States bonds can not be taxed by a State.

(3) "To regulate commerce with foreign nations, and among the several States, and with the Indian tribes."

(4) "To establish a uniform rule of naturalisation, and uniform laws on the subject of bankruptcies, throughout the United States."

(5) "To coin money; regulate the value thereof, and of foreign coin; and fix the standard of weights and measures."

(6) "To provide for the punishment of counterfeiting the securities and current coin of the United States."

(7) "To establish post-offices and post-roads."

(8) "To promote the progress of science and useful arts, by securing for limited times, to authors and inventors, the exclusive right to their respective writings and discoveries;"

That is, to grant copyrights to authors, and to issue patents to inventors.

(9) "To constitute tribunals inferior to the supreme court."

(10) "To define and punish piracies and felonies committed on the high seas, and offenses against the law of nations."

Piracy is robbery committed at sea.

(11) "To declare war; grant letters of marque and reprisal, and make rules concerning captures on land and water."

Letters of marque are commissions issued to private parties, authorizing them to cross the frontiers of another nation, and to seize the persons and property of its subjects.

Reprisal is the forcible taking of the property or persons of the subjects of another nation, in return for injuries done to the government granting the letters. Vessels carrying letters of marque and reprisal are called privateers.

(12) "To raise and support armies."

(13) "To provide and maintain a navy."

(14) "To make rules for the government and regulation of the land and naval forces."

(15) "To provide for calling forth the militia to execute the laws of the Union, suppress insurrection and repel invasions."

(16) "To provide for organizing, arming, and disciplining the militia, and for governing such part of them as may be employed in the service of the United States."

(17) "To exercise exclusive legislation" over the District of Columbia, "and to exercise like authority over all places purchased by the consent of the legislature of the State in which the same shall be, for the erection of forts,

magazines, arsenals, dockyards, and other needful buildings."

(18) "To make all laws which shall be necessary and proper for carrying into execution the foregoing powers and all other powers vested by this Constitution in the government of the United States, or in any department or officer thereof."

(19) "Congress may determine the time of choosing the electors" for President and Vice President of the United States, "and the day on which they shall give their votes, which day shall be the same throughout the United States."

(20) "Congress may, by law, provide for the case of removal, death, resignation, or inability of both the President and Vice President, declaring what officer shall then act as President."

(21) "The Congress may, by law, vest the appointment of such inferior officers as they think proper, in the President alone, in the courts of law, or in the heads of departments."

(22) "The Congress shall have power to declare the punishment of treason."

(23) "Full faith and credit shall be given in each State, to the public acts, records, and judicial proceedings of every other State. And the Congress may, by general laws, prescribe the manner in which such acts, records, and proceedings shall be proved, and the effect thereof."

(24) "New States may be admitted by the Congress into this Union, but no new State shall be formed or erected within the jurisdiction of any other State, nor any State be formed by the junction of two or more States, or parts of States, without the consent of the legislatures of the States concerned, as well as of the Congress."

(25) "The Congress shall have power to dispose of, and to make all needful rules and regulations respecting the territory or other property belonging to the United States; and nothing in this Constitution shall be so construed as to prejudice any claims of the United States or of any particular State."

(26) Congress has "power to enforce, by appropriate legislation," all provisions of the Constitution.

Under the authority "to provide for the general welfare of the United States," Congress exercises powers which are implied--that is, understood--but which are not expressly named in the Constitution. The grants of public lands to railway and canal companies, the annual appropriations for the improvement of rivers and harbors, and numerous similar laws are based upon implied powers.

FORBIDDEN POWERS.--The following powers are expressly denied to the national government:

(1) "The privilege of the writ of habeas corpus shall not be suspended unless when, in cases of rebellion or invasion, the public safety may require it."

Habeas corpus means "Thou mayst have the body." A person in prison, claiming to be unlawfully detained, or the friend of such a person, applies to the judge of a court for a writ of habeas corpus. The judge issues the writ, which directs the officer to bring the body of the prisoner into court at a certain time and place, in order that the legality of the imprisonment may be tested.

The case against the prisoner is not tried under the writ of habeas corpus, but the judge inquires whether any crime is charged, or whether there is a legal cause for the arrest. If the imprisonment is illegal, the judge orders the prisoner released; if the prisoner is lawfully held, the judge remands him to prison. This writ secures the freedom of every person unless detained upon legal charges. Therefore, there is no power in this wide country that can arrest and imprison even the humblest citizen except upon legal grounds. The writ of habeas corpus is the most famous writ known to the law, the strongest safeguard of the personal liberty of the citizens, and is regarded with almost a sacred reverence by the people.

(2) "No bill of attainder or ex post facto law shall be passed" by Congress.

A bill of attainder is an act of a legislative body inflicting the penalty of death without a regular trial. An ex post facto law is a law which fixes a penalty for acts done before the law was passed, or which increases the penalty of a crime after it is committed. Laws for punishing crime more severely can take effect only after their passage; they can not affect a crime committed before they were passed.

(3) "No tax or duty shall be laid on articles exported from any State. No preference shall be given, by any regulation of commerce or revenue, to the ports of one State over those of another; nor shall vessels bound to or from one State be obliged to enter, clear, or pay duties in another."

(4) "No money shall be drawn from the treasury but in consequence of appropriations made by law, and a regular statement and account of the receipts and expenditures of all public money shall be published from time to time."

(5) "No title of nobility shall be granted by the United States, and no person holding any office of profit or trust under them shall, without the consent of Congress, accept of any present, emolument, office, or title of any kind whatever, from any king, prince, or foreign State."

(6) "Congress shall make no law respecting establishment of religion, or prohibiting the free exercise thereof; or abridging the freedom of speech or of the press; or the right of the people peaceably to assemble, and to petition the government for a redress of grievances."

(7) "The validity of the public debt of the United States, authorized by law, including debts incurred for payment of pensions and bounties for services in suppressing insurrection or rebellion shall not be questioned. But neither the United States nor any State shall assume or pay any debt or obligation incurred in aid of insurrection or rebellion against the United States, or any claim for the loss or emancipation of any slave; but all such debts, obligations, and claims shall be held illegal and void."

The Constitution of the United States forbids the national government from exercising certain other powers, relating principally to slavery; but such denials are rendered useless by the freedom of the slaves.

THE UNITED STATES SENATE.

The Senate is composed of two senators from each State, elected by direct vote of the people;[1] and therefore each State has an equal representation, without regard to its area or the number of its people.

The term of a United States senator is six years, and one third of the Senate is elected every two years.

A senator must be thirty years old, for nine years a citizen of the United States, and must be an inhabitant of the State for which he shall be chosen.

A vacancy which occurs in any State's representation in the United States Senate is filled by an election for the unexpired term; but the legislature of any State may empower the governor to make temporary appointments until such election is held.

The Vice President of the United States is ex officio president of the Senate, but has no vote except when the Senate is equally divided upon a question. The Senate elects its other officers, including a president pro tempore, or temporary president, who presides when the Vice President is absent.

The Senate is a continuous body; that is, it is always organized, and when it meets it may proceed at once to business.

When the House of Representatives impeaches an officer of the United States, the impeachment is tried before the Senate sitting as a court.

The Senate has the sole power to try impeachments, and it requires two thirds of the senators present to convict. Judgment in cases of impeachment shall not extend further than to removal from office, and disqualification to hold and enjoy any office of honor, trust, or profit under the United States; but the party convicted shall, nevertheless, be liable and subject to indictment, trial, judgment, and punishment according to law.

All treaties made by the President of the United States with foreign countries must be laid before the Senate for ratification. If two thirds of the Senate vote for the treaty, it is ratified; otherwise, it is rejected.

Treaties are compacts or contracts between two or more nations made with a view to the public welfare of each, and are usually formed by agents or commissioners appointed by the respective governments of the countries concerned.

## HOUSE OF REPRESENTATIVES.

The House of Representatives, often called the lower House of Congress, is a much larger body than the Senate. The last apportionment of representatives, made in 1911, gave the House four hundred and thirty-five members, and this went into effect with the Sixty-third Congress, beginning on the 4th of March, 1913.

A census of the people is made every ten years, and upon this as a basis Congress fixes the number of representatives for the entire country, and the number to which each State shall be entitled for the next ten years thereafter. Each legislature divides the State into as many Congress districts as the State is entitled to representatives, and each district elects a representative by direct vote of the people.

The term of office is two years, and the terms of all representatives begin and end at the same time.

A representative must be twenty-five years old, must have been a citizen of the United States seven years, and must be an inhabitant of the State in which he is elected.

A vacancy in a State's representation in the lower house of Congress is filled by special election called by the governor for that purpose.

"All bills for raising revenue"--that is, all bills providing for taxation--"must originate in the House of Representatives; but the Senate may propose or concur with amendments, as in other bills." Taxation is called the strongest function of government, and therefore the Constitution provides that the first step must be taken by the House of Representatives, because all its members are elected every two years by the people, and are supposed to represent the people's views.

The Constitution provides that "the House of Representatives shall have the sole power of impeachment;" that is, the House of Representatives must formulate and present the charges to the Senate, and prosecute the accused at its bar. An impeachment by the House of Representatives corresponds to an indictment by a grand jury; specific charges must be made before a trial can be held in any court.

THE SPEAKER.--The speaker is elected by the representatives. He is a member of the House, and is nominated for the speakership by a convention, or caucus, of the representatives who are of his political party. In rank he is the third officer of the government. He presides over the House, preserves decorum, decides points of order, and directs the business of legislation. He is the organ of the House, and because he speaks and declares its will is called the Speaker. He formerly appointed the standing committees of the House, and thus largely shaped legislation; but this power was taken from him in 1911. As almost all laws are matured by the committees, and are passed as the result of their work, the power to appoint the committees was considered too important to leave in the hands of one man. The speaker's salary is $12,000 annually.

The clerk of the preceding House presides during the election of the speaker. Immediately after his election, the speaker is sworn into office by the representative of the longest service in the House. He then assumes the direction of business, and administers the oath to the members as they present themselves by States. The House of Representatives is reorganized every two years at the opening of the first session of each Congress.

OTHER OFFICERS.--The other officers of the House are the clerk, the sergeant-at-arms, the doorkeeper, the postmaster, and the chaplain. They are not members of the House. The sergeant-at-arms and the doorkeeper appoint numerous subordinates.

The sergeant-at-arms is the ministerial and police officer of the House. He preserves order, under the direction of the speaker, and executes all processes issued by the House or its committees. The symbol of authority of the House is the mace, consisting of a bundle of ebony rods surmounted by a globe, upon which is a silver eagle with outstretched wings. In scenes of disturbance, when the sergeant-at-arms bears the mace through the hall of the House at the speaker's command, the members immediately become quiet and order is restored.

The doorkeeper has charge of the hall of the House and its entrances. The postmaster receives and distributes the mail matter of the members. The chaplain opens the daily sessions of the House with prayer.

[1]After 1913. Before 1913 the senators of each State were elected by the legislature.

SUGGESTIVE QUESTIONS.

1. Why do not the people of the United States make their laws in person, instead of delegating this power to Congress?

2. Is it right that the President should hold the veto power?

3. Why is each House "judge of the elections, returns, and qualifications of its own members"?

4. Why are the yeas and nays entered on the Journal?

5. Why are senators and representatives privileged from arrest during the session, except for certain specified offenses?

6. Is it right to grant copyrights and patents?

7. What is counterfeiting?

8. Should United States senators be elected by the legislature or by the people?

9. How many senators in Congress now?

10. Who are the two United States senators from this State?

11. What is an impeachment?

12. How many representatives in Congress from this State?

13. Give the name of the representative from this district.

14. Who at present is speaker of the national House of Representatives?

15. Of what State is he a representative?

16. Name six of the most important committees of the House of Representatives.

QUESTION FOR DEBATE.

Resolved, That the members of the President's cabinet should be members of the House of Representatives.

CHAPTER XIII.

THE UNITED STATES--(Continued).

EXECUTIVE DEPARTMENT.

PRESIDENT: QUALIFICATIONS.--The executive power of the national government is vested in the President of the United States.

The President and the Vice President must be natural born citizens of this country, must have attained the age of thirty-five years, and must have resided fourteen years in the United States.

In case of the President's death, resignation, or removal from office, his duties devolve upon the Vice President; and if a vacancy occurs in the office, the Vice President becomes President of the United States. At other times the only duty of the Vice President is to preside over the Senate.

The President receives a salary of seventy-five thousand dollars per year; the annual salary of the Vice President is twelve thousand dollars.

ELECTION.--The President holds his office for a term of four years, and, together with the Vice President chosen for the same term, is elected in the following manner: During the earlier part of the regular year for the election of a President, each of the political parties in each state appoints delegates to the national convention of the party, either by means of conventions, or by vote at primary elections. Each party meets in national convention later on in the year, and nominates the candidates whom it will support for President and Vice President, and puts forth a declaration of principles called a "platform."

On Tuesday after the first Monday in November the people of the several States meet at their usual polling-places, and elect as many electors of President and Vice President as the State has senators and representatives in Congress. For this purpose candidates for electors have previously been nominated by the several parties naming candidates for President and Vice President.

The election returns are forwarded to the State capital, where they are compared, and the result declared by the election board of the State. The governor and secretary Of State issue certificates to the persons chosen as electors of President and Vice President.

On the second Monday in January the electors of each State meet at the State capital and cast their votes for the candidates of their party for President and Vice President. They make, sign, certify, and seal three separate lists of their votes for President and Vice President; transmit two lists to the president of the United States Senate--one by mail and the other by special messenger--and file the remaining list with the judge of the United States district court of the district in which the electors meet.

On the second Wednesday in February the United States Senate and House of Representatives meet in joint session. The president of the Senate opens the certificates of votes from all the States, and the votes are then counted. The person having the highest number of votes for President is declared elected President, if his votes are a majority of all the electors elected in the whole Union.

If no person receives a majority of all the electoral votes, then the House of Representatives elects the President from the three candidates receiving the highest numbers of votes. A quorum for the purpose is a representative or representatives from two thirds of the States. Each State has one vote, cast as a majority of its representatives present directs; and a majority of ail the States is necessary to elect.

The person receiving the highest number of votes for Vice President is elected Vice President, if his votes are a majority of the whole number of electors chosen.

If his votes are not a majority of all the electors, then the Senate proceeds to elect the Vice President from the two candidates receiving the highest number of votes for Vice President. A quorum for the purpose consists of two thirds of the senators from all the States. Each senator has one vote, and a majority of the whole number is necessary to elect.

The people do not vote directly for President and Vice President, but for electors by whom the President and the Vice President are chosen. The electors of all the States are called collectively the electoral college.

The electors may vote for some other person than the candidate nominated by their respective parties; but no elector has ever chosen to exercise this privilege. They consider themselves in honor pledged and instructed to cast their votes for the candidate of their own political faith.

The vote of the people for electors is called the popular vote, and the vote of the electors for President is called the electoral vote. As has several times happened in our history, a candidate may be elected President or Vice President and yet be in a minority of the popular vote.

INAUGURATION.--On the 4th of March following the election the President and the Vice President assume the duties of their respective offices amid imposing ceremonies.

The Vice President is first sworn into office in the presence of the United States Senate. The following oath of office is then administered to the President-elect by the Chief Justice of the United States Supreme Court: "I do solemnly swear (or affirm) that I will faithfully execute the office of President of the United States; and will, to the best of my ability, preserve, protect, and defend the Constitution of the United States."

In the presence of a vast concourse of citizens the President delivers an address, outlining the public policy to be pursued during his term of office. There is usually a display of civil and military organizations representing all sections of the country. The political differences of the people are in great part forgotten in the enthusiasm attending the inauguration of the President.

OFFICIAL RESIDENCE.--The presidential mansion in the city of Washington is called the White House. It was erected and is maintained by the national government at public expense. Here the President resides with his family, and receives private citizens, members of Congress, officers of other departments of the government, and foreign ministers and dignitaries.

At his public receptions, held at stated times, he may be called upon by the humblest person in the land. This shows the spirit of equality which prevails even in the highest station under our system of government. Our institutions are based upon the principle embodied in the Declaration of Independence, "That all men are created equal."

DIGNITY AND RESPONSIBILITY.--The office of President of the United States is the highest in the gift of the people. "He represents the unity, power, and purpose of the nation." He is the first citizen of the United States, holding the position of highest dignity, influence, and responsibility in the whole country. He directs the machinery of the government, and is therefore held responsible by the people for the conduct of public affairs, and largely for the condition of the country.

His term of office is called an administration. He and his official advisers have the appointment of more than one hundred and fifteen thousand officers of the national government.

MESSAGES.--At the opening of each regular session of Congress the President sends or delivers to both houses his annual message, in which he reviews events of the previous year, gives "information of the state of the Union," and recommends the passage of such laws as he deems "necessary and expedient." From time to time he gives information upon special subjects, and recommends the passage of measures of pressing importance. The heads of departments make yearly reports to the President, which are printed for the information of Congress.

DUTIES AND POWERS.--The duties of the President are so extensive, the burdens of his office so heavy, and his power so great, that the people believe that no man, however wise and eminent, should hold the office for more than two terms. Washington set the example of voluntary retirement at the end of the second term, and it seems to be an unwritten law that no President shall serve more than eight years in succession. The duties of the office, so various and so burdensome, are summed up in the provision of the Constitution: "He shall take care that the laws be faithfully executed."

The President approves or vetoes all bills and joint-resolutions passed by Congress, except those relating to questions of adjournment. All measures vetoed must, within ten days after they are received, be returned to the house in which they originated. The power to veto acts of Congress is called the legislative power of the President.

He is commander-in-chief of the army and the navy of the United States, and of the militia of the several States when engaged in the national service. He does not command in person, but places the forces under the orders of officers of his choice.

He may require information in writing from the heads of departments upon subjects relating to their respective offices. As he appoints these officers, and may remove them at his pleasure, the people hold him responsible for their official conduct. He is held responsible for the official actions of all officers of the executive department of the government.

He may grant reprieves and pardons for offenses against the United States, except in cases of impeachment. Frequent appeals are made to his pardoning power.

He may make treaties with foreign countries, but before a treaty can have any effect it must be submitted by him to the Senate, and must be ratified by a vote of two thirds of the senators present. With the consent of the Senate, he appoints ministers to foreign courts, consuls to foreign countries, judges of the United States Supreme Court, and other officers, of the national government. He fills vacancies in office which occur during recesses of the Senate, by granting commissions which expire at the close of the next session of the Senate.

He may, in cases of extreme necessity, call special session of Congress, or of either house. If the Senate and the House of Representatives fail to agree upon a time to which they shall adjourn, the President may adjourn them to such time as he may think proper. Such a necessity has never arisen, and therefore this power has never been exercised.

The President may receive or refuse to receive ministers and other agents of foreign governments. To receive a minister is to recognize the nation which he represents. He may also dismiss foreign ministers who do not prove acceptable to our government.

He commissions all officers of the United States. The power to make appointments of office is called his patronage. A civil service commission, consisting of three commissioners, has been established by act of Congress, to secure efficiency in the public service, and to prevent the appointment of men to office as a reward for party work. Before applicants for certain offices can be appointed they must pass an examination prescribed by the civil service commission.

## CABINET.

The President's cabinet is a council of ten official advisers, appointed by him and confirmed by the Senate. They are often called heads of departments. The members of the cabinet are the secretary of state, secretary of the treasury, secretary of war, secretary of the navy, postmaster-general, secretary of the interior, attorney-general, secretary of agriculture, secretary of commerce, and secretary of labor.

They may be removed by the President at pleasure, and are directly responsible to him for the conduct of their respective departments. The President holds frequent meetings of the cabinet for the purpose of conferring upon official business; but he may, if he choose, disregard their advice and act upon his own judgment.

In case of the death, resignation, removal, or disability of both President and Vice President, the presidential office would be filled by a member of the cabinet, in this order: The secretary of state, the secretary of the treasury, the secretary of war, the attorney-general, the postmaster-general, the secretary of the navy, the secretary of the interior.

Each of the cabinet officers receives a salary of twelve thousand dollars per year.

DEPARTMENT OF STATE.--The secretary of state is the head of the department of state, formerly called the department of foreign affairs. His office is the highest rank in the cabinet, and is next in importance to that of the President. He preserves the original draughts of all treaties, laws, public documents, and correspondence with foreign countries. He keeps the great seal of the United States, and fixes it to all commissions signed by the President. He furnishes copies of records and papers kept in his office, impressed with the seal of his department, and authenticates all proclamations and messages of the President.

He has charge of the negotiation of treaties and other foreign affairs, conducts correspondence with foreign ministers, issues instructions for the guidance of our ministers and other agents to foreign countries, and from time to time reports to Congress the relations of the United States with other governments. He is the organ of communication between the President and the governors of the States.

He issues traveling papers, called passports, to citizens wishing to travel in foreign countries. When foreign criminals take refuge in this country, he issues warrants for their delivery according to the terms of existing treaties. He presents to the President all foreign ministers, and is the only officer authorized to represent him in correspondence with foreign governments.

The secretary of state has three assistants, called respectively, first assistant secretary of state, second assistant secretary of state, and third assistant secretary of state.

The department of state conducts the foreign affairs of the government chiefly through the diplomatic service and the consular service.

THE DIPLOMATIC SERVICE.--The officers of the diplomatic service are called ministers, and represent the United States in a political capacity. They negotiate treaties under the direction of the secretary of state, and maintain friendly relations between the United States and the countries to which they are accredited. They are forbidden to engage in any commercial transaction, or to exercise any control over the commercial interests of the United States.

By the laws of nations, foreign ministers in all countries enjoy many rights and privileges not accorded to other foreign persons. They are assisted by interpreters, who explain speeches made in foreign tongues; and by secretaries of legation, who keep the records, and attend to the minor duties of the ministers.

The diplomatic service consists of ambassadors extraordinary and plenipotentiary, of envoys extraordinary and ministers plenipotentiary, and of ministers resident. These officials rank in the order named, but the duties are the same; the chief difference being in the rank and influence of the countries to which they are accredited.

The ambassadors and ministers of the higher rank receive salaries ranging from seven thousand five hundred dollars to seventeen thousand five hundred dollars each, the latter sum being paid to the ambassadors to such important countries as Great Britain, Germany, France, Russia, Mexico, Japan, etc.

There are very few ministers resident. They generally serve also as consuls general, and receive from four thousand dollars to seven thousand dollars each. Ministers sent to foreign countries upon special service, such as the negotiation of special treaties, are sometimes called commissioners.

CONSULAR SERVICE.--The consular service includes about sixty consuls general, some of whom are inspectors of consulates, about two hundred and fifty consuls, and many deputies and other assistants.

The chief duties of consuls are to enforce the commercial laws, and to protect the rights of American citizens. Consuls reside at the principal cities of the consular districts to which they are accredited. The interests of American shipping and American seamen are specially intrusted to their care. They keep the papers of American vessels while in port; they record the tonnage, the kind and value of the cargo, and the number and condition of the sailors. They hear the complaints of seamen, cause the arrest of mutinous sailors, send them home for trial, and care for mariners in destitute condition. They take possession of the property of American citizens dying abroad, and forward the proceeds to the lawful heirs.

They collect valuable information relating to the commerce and manufactures of foreign countries, which is distributed among our people by the department of commerce.

In Turkey and China, American citizens who are charged with crime are tried by the American consul. Consuls and consuls general receive salaries ranging from two thousand dollars to twelve thousand dollars each, according to the importance of the cities where they are located.

TREASURY DEPARTMENT.--The secretary of the treasury is the head of the treasury department. He manages the entire financial system of the national government. He suggests to Congress plans for raising revenue and maintaining the credit of the United States, and makes detailed reports on all the operations of his department.

He superintends the collection of revenue; the coinage of money; the operation of national banks; the conduct of custom-houses, where taxes on imported foreign goods are collected. The schedule or table showing the duties levied on foreign goods is called the tariff; this is fixed by act of Congress. The management of the public health service, and the operation of the coast guard, maintained along the seacoast for the rescue of persons from drowning and for the enforcement of navigation laws, are also under the charge of the secretary of the treasury. His greatest responsibility is the management of the national debt, which still amounts to many hundred millions of dollars.

BUREAUS.--The secretary of the treasury is assisted by three assistant secretaries of the treasury, a comptroller, six auditors, a treasurer, a register of the treasury, and numerous other responsible officers in charge of the bank currency, internal revenue, the mint, the erection of public buildings, and other important bureaus and divisions of the treasury department.

The comptroller directs the work of the six auditors, and superintends the recovery of debts due the United States.

The auditor for the treasury department settles--that is, examines and passes on--all accounts in the collection of customs duties and internal revenue, the national debt, and other accounts immediately connected with the operations of the treasury department.

The auditor for the war department settles the army accounts.

The auditor for the interior department settles pension accounts, accounts with the Indians, and all other accounts arising in the department of the interior.

The auditor for the navy department settles the accounts of the navy.

The auditor for the state and other departments has charge of the accounts of the secretary of state, the attorney-general, the secretary of agriculture, the secretary of commerce, and the secretary of labor, and of all the officials under their direction; the accounts of the United States courts; and those of various institutions which are not under the control of any department.

The auditor for the post-office department examines and passes on the accounts of the postal service.

The treasurer is custodian of the funds of the United States. All funds and securities are kept in vaults made for the purpose, or deposited in reliable banks for safe keeping.

The register of the treasury has charge of the account-books of United States bonds and paper money. They show the exact financial condition of the United States at all times. The register's name is upon all bonds and notes issued by the government.

The comptroller of the currency supervises the national banks. A bank is a place for the safe keeping and lending of money. A bank holding its charter-- that is, its power to do business--from a State government is called a State bank. Two kinds of banks are chartered by the national government: the national banks and the federal reserve banks.

By the laws of the United States, any five or more persons with sufficient capital may organize a national bank. A national bank may issue its notes--that is, its promises to pay--as currency, to an amount not exceeding the amount of United States bonds deposited by the bank with the national government. Each federal reserve bank is a large central bank organized by the banks of a certain district. It issues notes as currency, secured by commercial notes, drafts, etc.

The commissioner of internal revenue supervises the collection of income taxes and of taxes laid upon tobacco; liquors, etc., manufactured in this country.

The director of the mint has charge of the coinage of money, and reports to Congress upon the yield of precious metals. There are mints at Philadelphia, Carson, San Francisco, Denver, and New Orleans, and assay offices also at other places.

The Constitution vests the power to coin money in the national government alone.

The director of the bureau of engraving and printing supervises the execution of designs and the engraving and printing of revenue and postage stamps, national bank notes, and the notes, bonds, and other financial paper of the United States.

The supervising architect selects plans for the erection of custom-houses, court-houses, post-offices, mints, and other public buildings of the United States.

The surgeon-general of the public health service has charge of the marine hospitals, and helps to enforce the laws which aim to prevent the introduction of contagious diseases into the country. He calls conferences of state health boards.

The solicitor of the treasury is the chief lawyer for the department. He has charge of prosecutions for violations of the customs laws, and other crimes against the financial interests of the United States. Like similar lawyers for other departments, he is included in the department of justice, under the attorney-general.

WAR DEPARTMENT.--The secretary of war is the head of the war department. He has charge of the land forces, under the direction of the President. He supervises the expenditure of money voted by Congress for the improvement of rivers and harbors, and for the United States Military Academy at West Point, as well as for the support and operations of the army. In the management of his department he is aided by an assistant secretary of war.

BUREAUS.--The war department has numerous offices and bureaus, each in the charge of a responsible officer, and all under the supervision of the Chief of Staff, who is the military adviser of the secretary of war.

The adjutant-general issues the military orders of his superiors, conducts the army correspondence, issues commissions, and keeps the army records.

The quartermaster-general provides quarters, food, clothing, and transportation for the army, and has charge of barracks and national cemeteries. He also supervises the payment of the army and the military academy.

The surgeon-general superintends the army hospitals, and the distribution of medical stores for the army.

The inspector-general attends to inspection of the arms and equipments of the soldiers.

The chief of engineers supervises the construction of forts, the improvement of rivers and harbors, and the surveys relating to them.

The chief of ordnance furnishes guns and ammunition to the army and to forts, and has charge of armories and arsenals.

The judge-advocate-general, who is chief of the bureau of military justice, prosecutes crimes committed in the army, and reviews all sentences passed by military courts and military commissions.

MILITARY ACADEMY.--The military academy at West Point is maintained for the education of officers for the army. Each member of Congress appoints two cadets to the academy, and the President appoints four from the District of Columbia and eighty from the United States at large. There are also appointed two from each territory, two from Porto Rico, and a certain number of enlisted men from the army. The academy is under the charge of an army officer, appointed by the secretary of war. Each cadet receives from the government an allowance sufficient to pay all necessary expenses.

NAVY DEPARTMENT.--The secretary of the navy presides over the navy department. He has control of all affairs relating to vessels of war, the naval forces, and naval operations. He has charge of the Naval Observatory at Washington, and of the United States Naval Academy at Annapolis. There is an assistant secretary of the navy.

The naval department issues sailing charts, sailing directions, and other publications for the use of seamen. Among these is the nautical almanac used in navigating ships.

BUREAUS.--The naval department has a number of bureaus, which are in charge of competent officers detailed from the naval service.

The bureau of navigation gives out and enforces the secretary's orders to the officers of the navy, enlists sailors, keeps the records of the service, and has charge of the naval academy. It has charge of the training and education of line officers and enlisted men of the navy.

The bureau of yards and docks attends to the navy yards, docks, wharves, their buildings and machinery.

The bureau of ordnance superintends the forging and testing of cannon, guns, and other military equipments, and the construction of naval torpedoes.

The bureau of medicine and surgery has charge of the naval laboratory, the eight naval hospitals, and the purchase and distribution of surgical instruments and medical stores for the naval department.

The bureau of supplies and accounts purchases and distributes provisions and clothing for the navy.

The bureau of steam engineering superintends the construction and repair of engines and machinery for the vessels of war.

The bureau of construction and repair has charge of all matters relating to the construction and repair of all vessels and boats used in the naval service.

NAVAL ACADEMY.--The naval academy at Annapolis is maintained by the national government for the purpose of educating and training officers for the navy. It bears the same relation to the navy that the military academy bears to the army. At the academy there are three midshipmen for each member of Congress; the President appoints two from the District of Columbia and ten a year from the United States at large; and fifteen enlisted men of the navy are appointed each year on competitive examination. The academy is under the charge of a superintendent, appointed by the secretary of the navy. Each midshipman receives from the government an annual sum of money sufficient to pay all necessary expenses incurred at the academy.

POST-OFFICE DEPARTMENT.--The postmaster-general presides over the post-office department. He has control of all questions relating to the management of post-offices and the carrying of the mails, and appoints all postmasters whose annual salaries are less than a thousand dollars each. Postmasters whose salaries exceed this sum are appointed by the President of the United States.

BUREAUS.--The postmaster-general has four assistants, who, under him, are in charge of the various details of the vast establishment devoted to the postal service.

The first assistant postmaster-general has general charge of post-offices and postmasters, and makes preparations for the appointment of all postmasters. He also controls the free delivery of mail matter in cities, and the dead letter office.

The second assistant postmaster-general attends to the letting of contracts for carrying the mails, decides upon the mode of conveyance, and fixes the time for the arrival and departure of mails at each post-office. He also has charge of the foreign mail service. The United States has postal treaties with all the other civilized countries in the world, by which regular mail lines are maintained.

The third assistant postmaster-general has charge of financial matters. He provides stamps, stamped envelopes, and postal cards for post-offices, and receives the reports and settlements of postmasters. He also superintends the registered mail service, the postal savings system, and the post-office money-order business. By means of money orders people may deposit money in the post-office at which they mail their letters, and have it paid at the office to which their letters are addressed.

The fourth assistant postmaster-general has charge of the rural free delivery system,--a very important service. He also furnishes blanks and stationery to post-offices throughout the United States, and supervises the making of the various post-route maps, such as those used for rural delivery and for the parcel post.

INTERIOR DEPARTMENT.--The secretary of the interior is the chief officer of the interior department. The former name, home department, suggests the character of the subjects under its control. Its duties relate to various public interests which have been transferred to it from other departments. The department of the interior has charge of pensions, public lands, Indian affairs, patents, education, and the geological survey.

The commissioner of pensions has charge of the examination of pension claims and the granting of pensions and bounties for service in the army and the navy. There are about a million names on the pension rolls of the United States, and the annual payment of pensions amounts to about one hundred and forty million dollars.

The commissioner of the general land office superintends the surveys and sales of the lands belonging to the national government. The United States surveys divide the public lands into ranges, townships, sections, and fractions of sections. Ranges are bounded by north and south lines, six miles apart, and are numbered east and west. Ranges are divided into townships, each six miles square, numbered north and south. A township is divided into thirty-six sections, each one mile square, and containing six hundred and forty acres of land; and sections are divided into quarter sections.

The commissioner of Indian affairs has charge of questions relating to the government of the Indians. Its agents make treaties, manage lands, issue rations and clothing, and conduct trade with the Indians.

The commissioner of patents conducts all matters pertaining to the granting of patents for useful inventions, discoveries, and improvements.

A patent gives the inventor the exclusive right to manufacture, sell, and use the patented article for a period of seventeen years.

A copyright, which is somewhat similar to a patent, gives the author of a book the exclusive right to print, publish, and sell it for a period of twenty-eight years, with the privilege at the expiration of that time of renewing for twenty-eight years more.

An inventor or author may sell a patent or copyright, as well as other property.

The commissioner of education investigates the condition and progress of education in the several States and Territories, and collects information relating to schools, school systems, and methods of teaching. The facts collected are distributed among the people in annual reports published by the office.

The director of the geological survey sends out parties of scientific men, who explore various parts of the Union, trace the sources of rivers, measure the heights of lands, and gather other facts relating to the natural resources of the country. He publishes excellent maps of the regions that have been explored.

DEPARTMENT OF JUSTICE.--The attorney-general presides over the department of justice. He is the chief law officer of the government, and the legal adviser of all the departments. He is assisted by the solicitor-general, who is the second officer in rank; by nine assistant attorney-generals, and by several solicitors for particular departments. The department of justice conducts before the supreme court all suits to which the United States is a party; conducts suits arising in any of the departments, when requested by the head thereof; exercises supervision over the district attorneys and marshals of the United States district courts; examines the titles of lands proposed to be purchased by the United States, as sites for forts, arsenals, barracks, dockyards, customhouses, post-offices, and other public purposes; examines and reports upon applications for judicial offices and other positions requiring legal ability.

DEPARTMENT OF AGRICULTURE.--The department of agriculture was reorganized in 1889. Previous to that time it had been a bureau of the interior department. The secretary of agriculture is the chief officer of the department of agriculture.

This department collects and diffuses among the people useful knowledge relating to agriculture and agricultural products. Experiments are conducted upon farm and garden products, and the seeds of choice varieties are distributed among the people. Similar attention is given to stock-raising and the care of forests. The bureau of chemistry assists in the enforcement of the pure food law.

The department also includes the weather bureau, which collects and publishes telegraphic reports of storms and the condition of the weather, in the interest of agriculture and commerce.

DEPARTMENT OF COMMERCE.--The department of commerce and labor was created in 1903, and ten years later was divided into two departments. The secretary of commerce presides over the department of commerce. Its duty is to promote and develop commerce, mining, manufacturing, and fisheries. It collects and publishes facts and figures on all these subjects; supplies exactly true weights and measures for any one to copy; controls stations for stocking waters with valuable fish; inspects and licenses steamships, rejecting any that are unseaworthy; surveys the seacoast of the United States, and maintains lighthouses at dangerous points.

The work of the department is divided among a number of bureaus, many of which were already in existence when the new department was formed. Among these is the census office, which takes a census of the United States every ten years, besides collecting other statistics at shorter intervals.

DEPARTMENT OF LABOR.--The secretary of labor presides over the department of labor. Its duty is to promote the welfare of wage earners. It makes important investigations, and publishes statistics concerning laborers. This department includes the children's bureau, which studies problems, affecting children's welfare. It also includes the bureau of immigration and the bureau of naturalisation, which supervise the enforcement of United States laws regarding immigration and naturalization.

SEPARATE COMMISSIONS.--In addition to the civil service commission, Congress has created two other important commissions not connected with any department. The interstate commerce commission, consisting of seven members appointed by the President, supervises interstate railroads, express companies, etc., and enforces the laws which control them. The federal trade commission, consisting of five members appointed by the President, supervises the business of persons and companies engaged in interstate commerce, except those under the control of the interstate commerce commission.

SUGGESTIVE QUESTIONS.

1. Why does the Constitution require that the President shall be a native of the United States?

2. Who is now President, and of what State is he a citizen?

3. When was he elected?

4. Should the President be eligible for reelection?

5. Do you think he should have the veto power?

6. Of what use is a passport in traveling?

7. What is internal revenue?

8. What was the principal cause of the national debt?

9. How many soldiers, including officers, in the army of the United States?

10. Of what value are the weather reports?

11. Why is it right for the government to grant pensions?

12. Why should a census be taken?

13. What is the population of the United States, and what the population of this State, by the last census?

14. What is meant by conducting a suit before the supreme court?

QUESTION FOR DEBATE.

Resolved, That the President and the Vice President should be elected by the popular vote.

CHAPTER XIV.

THE UNITED STATES--(Continued).

JUDICIAL DEPARTMENT.

The judicial department is one of the three great departments of the government, being coordinate with Congress, the legislative power, and with the President, the executive power. The principle of three coordinate departments of government is new, the United States being the first nation that ever embodied it in its constitution.

The judicial system of the United States includes the Supreme Court of the United States, the circuit courts of appeals, district courts, the courts of the District of Columbia, the court of claims, the court of customs appeals, a territorial court for each of the Territories, and several commissioners' courts in each of the States.

JURISDICTION OF UNITED STATES COURTS.--The jurisdiction of United States courts extends to the following classes of suits at law:

1. To all cases arising under laws passed by Congress.

2. Those affecting ministers, consuls, and other agents of the United States and foreign countries.

3. Suits arising on the high seas.

4. All suits to which the United States is a party.

5. Controversies between a State and the citizens of another State.

6. Cases between citizens of different States.

7. Suits between citizens of the same State claiming lands under grants by different States.

8. Cases between a State or its citizens and a foreign State or its citizens.

It will be seen that all cases at law to which a State is a party must be tried in the courts of the United States. A direct suit can not be brought against the United States except by authority of a special act of Congress; nor can a suit be brought against a State by a citizen of another State, or by one of its own citizens, except by the special permission of its legislature.

SUPREME COURT OF THE UNITED STATES.--The Supreme Court of the United States is the highest judicial tribunal in the country. It consists of the Chief Justice and eight associate justices, nominated by the President and confirmed by the Senate. The country is divided into nine circuits, each represented by a Justice of the Supreme Court. The justices hold their offices during life, unless impeached; but they have the privilege of retiring upon full pay, at seventy years of age, provided they have served in the court for ten years. A quorum consists of any six justices, and if a majority agree upon a decision it becomes the decision of the court.

The court holds annual sessions in the Capitol building at Washington, beginning upon the second Monday in October. The annual salary of the Chief Justice is fifteen thousand dollars; that of the associate justices is fourteen thousand five hundred dollars each.

The Constitution of the United States creates and names the Supreme Court, and provides that the Judicial power shall be vested in it "and in such inferior courts as the Congress may from time to time ordain and establish."

JURISDICTION.--The Supreme Court has original jurisdiction in all cases affecting ministers, consuls, and other agents of the United States and foreign countries, and in cases to which a State is a party.

Most cases tried by it are brought before it upon appeals from the inferior courts of the United States. They involve chiefly the questions of jurisdiction of the inferior courts, the constitutionality of laws, the validity of treaties, and the sentences in criminal and prize causes. An appeal from a State court can be carried to the Supreme Court only upon the ground that the decision of the State court is in conflict with the Constitution or laws of the United States.

The peculiar province of the Supreme Court is to interpret the Constitution, and in all conflicts between a State and the nation the final decision rests with the Supreme Court of the United States. It may, and does, modify its own judgments; but until it modifies or reverses a decision, it is final, and from it there is no appeal. Whether its decree be against a private citizen, a State, the Congress, or the President, that decree is "the end of the whole matter," and must be obeyed.

The Supreme Court is more admired and praised by foreign critics than is any other of our institutions. It is conceded by all to be one of the strongest and best features in our system of government. In a free country like ours, such a tribunal is necessary to prevent the legislative and executive departments from trespassing upon the Constitution, and invading the rights of the people. Therefore the Supreme Court of the United States has been appropriately called "the balance-wheel in our system of government."

UNITED STATES CIRCUIT COURTS OF APPEALS.--Each United States circuit embraces several States, and has two or more circuit judges. One justice of the Supreme Court is also assigned to each circuit. There are nine circuit courts of appeals, one for each United States circuit. All appeals from the district courts must be made to the circuit courts of appeals, except in cases expressly provided by law to be taken direct to the Supreme Court; but provision is also made for appeal from the decision of the circuit courts of appeals to the Supreme Court in certain classes of cases.

UNITED STATES DISTRICT COURT.--Each State has one or more United States district courts, each presided over by a district judge. The district court has both civil and criminal jurisdiction in all cases under the national law which are not required to be brought in other courts. Before 1912 there were so-called "circuit courts" usually held by the district judges, for the trial of certain important kinds of cases; but these were abolished by an act of 1911.

In each State a large majority of the civil and criminal cases must be tried and finally decided in the State courts. However, among the important cases tried in United States courts are those concerning patents, copyrights, and bankruptcy, those involved in the regulation of interstate and foreign commerce, and offenses committed against the postal and revenue laws.

Interstate commerce cases are often in the form of appeals from the orders issued by the interstate commerce commission, fixing the freight and passenger rates of railroads, etc. Such a case is heard by three judges sitting together, and an appeal from their decision can be taken directly to the Supreme Court.

If the circuit and district judges desire, they may retire upon full pay at the age of seventy, after ten years of consecutive service.

COURT OF CUSTOMS APPEALS.--The customs court consists of a chief judge and four associate judges. It decides disputes over the rates of duty payable on imported goods. It holds sessions both at Washington and in other cities.

COURT OF CLAIMS.--The court of claims holds its sessions at Washington, and consists of a chief justice and four associate justices. It hears and determines claims against the United States. No one could bring suit against the national government without permission from Congress; but a person having a claim against it may submit the claim to the court of claims for trial, and, if the claim is declared to be legal and just, it is almost always paid by act of Congress.

OTHER COURTS.--The District of Columbia has six supreme court justices and three justices of a court of appeals. Their jurisdiction is similar to that of the United States district courts and circuit courts of appeals, but is confined to the District of Columbia.

Territorial courts consist of a chief justice and two associate justices, who hold their offices for a term of four years, unless removed by the President. A territorial court holds its sessions in the Territory for which it is constituted, and has jurisdiction of cases arising under the laws of Congress and the laws passed by the territorial legislature.

Appeals are taken from the courts of the District of Columbia and from the territorial courts to the supreme court of the United States.

A United States commissioner's court consists of a commissioner appointed by the judge of the district court. The chief duties of this court are to arrest and hold for trial persons charged with offenses against the United States, and to assist in taking testimony for the trial of cases. A judge of a State court or a justice of the peace may act as United States commissioner, but while engaged in such duties he is an officer of the United States, and not of the State.

TERM OF SERVICE.--Justices of circuit courts, district courts, the customs court, the court of claims, the courts of the District of Columbia, and of the territorial courts, are appointed by the President and confirmed by the Senate. The justices of these courts, except of the territorial courts, hold their offices during life, unless impeached. This life tenure of office, and the provision that a salary of a justice shall not be reduced during his term, render the courts of the United States independent of Congress and public opinion, and tend to preserve the purity and dignity of their decisions.

The salary of a judge of the circuit court is seven thousand dollars; that of a judge of a district court is six thousand dollars; that of a judge of the customs court is seven thousand dollars; and that of a justice of the court of claims is six thousand dollars, except the chief justice, who receives six thousand five hundred dollars.

OFFICERS OF COURTS.--The United States district courts have grand juries and trial juries, who perform duties similar to those of juries in State courts. With the consent of the Senate, the President appoints for each district a United States district attorney and a United States marshal.

The district attorney represents the United States in all civil cases to which it is a party, and is the prosecuting officer in criminal cases.

The marshal is the executive and ministerial officer of the court, with duties similar to those of a sheriff.

The Supreme Court of the United States appoints a reporter, who reports--that is, edits and publishes--its decisions. This court also appoints its own marshal. The decisions of the district court are reported by the Judge, or by an attorney under the judge's sanction. Each court appoints a clerk, who keeps a record of its proceedings; gives a history of each case; notes all orders, decisions, and judgments; has charge of all money paid; and keeps and fixes the seal of the court.

The circuit courts of appeals appoint their own marshals and clerks. The duties of these officers are similar to those performed by the marshal and clerk of the Supreme Court. The circuit courts of appeals have no reporters.

SUGGESTIVE QUESTIONS.

1. Who is chief justice of the United States, and of what State is he a citizen?

2. Why should a judge hold his position during a long term of years?

3. This State is a part of what United States circuit?

4. What justice represents this circuit in the supreme court?

5. Who is judge of the United States district court of this district?

6. Why can no person bring suit against the United States except by special act of Congress?

QUESTION FOR DEBATE.

Resolved, That the jury system should be abolished.

PART II.

CHAPTER XV.

# GOVERNMENT.

Government is defined as rule or control. It is that which governs, and also the act of governing. In its political sense, it means the supreme authority of a State or other political community, or the act by which this authority is applied. It is sometimes said to be a system of institutions for the restraint of people living in the social state or social condition.

The word govern is derived from a Latin word which first meant to steer the ship, and then very naturally came to mean to guide, to direct, to command.

"The comparison of governing with steering is a very happy one," for the interest of him who steers is the same as that of the people in the ship: "all must float or sink together." So the interest of those that govern, of those that guide "the ship of state," as we often express it, is the same as that of the people.[1]

ORIGIN AND NECESSITY.--The origin of government is unknown; its beginning can not be traced. People everywhere, in all the varying degrees of civilization, recognize the necessity of a supreme authority, to whom all owe and render obedience.

Men can not long live in the same vicinity without some kind of political organization. Without some sort of government--that is, some supreme power to settle disputes--the people would be in continual warfare; there could be no security to person or property; each individual could look to himself alone for safety; "his hand would be against every man, and every man's hand against him."

Wherever men are found they live under some form of government, however rude and imperfect. In all parts and in all ages of the world they have seen the necessity of some power to protect the weak and restrain the strong, and have therefore set up a supreme authority for the common welfare.

A body of people living under government is called society, and the agreement existing between them, for their common welfare, is called the social compact.

Men are so constituted that society is necessary to their happiness. Therefore they seek the social state and join the social compact, thus agreeing to be governed by law and order.

FOR THE PEOPLE.--Government is for the people, and not for the rulers. Officers, the highest and the lowest, are merely the servants of the people.

All governments derive their just powers from the consent of the people, and are established and maintained for their good. All powers which are exercised without the consent of the people are unjust and tyrannical.

KINDS.--Government is of two kinds, civil and military.

Civil government is the government of civil society, or the government of the people in a peaceful state.

Military government is the government of men in a state of war. It prevails in the army and the navy, and sometimes in districts which are the scenes of military operations.

Military government is conducted by the rules of martial law, and in its penalties and exactions is much more severe than civil government.

FORMS OF CIVIL GOVERNMENT.

There are many forms of civil government, but they may be reduced to three principal systems:

1. Monarchy: government by one person.

2. Aristocracy: government by a few persons.

3. Democracy: government by the people.

Every government is either one of these forms or is composed of two or more of them.

MONARCHY.--A monarchy is a government whose chief authority is vested in one person, usually called king, queen, emperor, empress, or prince. Monarchies are absolute or limited.

In an absolute monarchy there is no limit to the power of the monarch; his wishes are the laws of the people. The people are his property, and in his person are combined all the powers of government, legislative, executive, and judicial. Russia is the only civilized nation whose government is still an absolute monarchy.

In a constitutional monarchy the sovereign, or chief ruler, must govern by laws made by a representative body elected by the people. England and Germany are constitutional monarchies.

In an hereditary monarchy the sovereign inherits the ruling power, usually from his father.

In an elective monarchy the sovereign is elected for life, usually by the dignitaries of other nations.

A patriarchy is a monarchy in which the chief power is exercised by a patriarch, or father. The authority of the patriarch is confined to his tribe. This form of government was common in ancient times, before tribes were combined into nations.

A theocracy is a monarchy whose rulers claim to be under the direct guidance of God. The government of the ancient Hebrews was a theocracy.

ARISTOCRACY.--An aristocracy, sometimes called oligarchy, is a government in which the supreme authority is vested in a privileged few, distinguished by their wealth and social position.

The privileged class are usually called nobles. They are above the common people in rank and bear titles of honor. These titles are mostly inherited, but are sometimes conferred upon persons by the sovereign.

An aristocracy never exists by itself; it is always combined with some other form of government, usually with a constitutional monarchy. The government of England is partly aristocratic; the House of Lords, one of the bodies of

Parliament, being composed of nobles.

DEMOCRACY.--A democracy is a "government of the people, by the people, for the people." It is a government by many, instead of by one or by a few. Hereditary titles are inconsistent with democratic government, and therefore never exist in a democracy.

A pure democracy is a government conducted by the people in person. It is practicable only in a political community so small that all the people may assemble at the seat of government. The New England "town meeting" is almost the only example of a pure democracy in the world at the present time; certainly the only example in the United States.

A republic, or representative democracy, is a government conducted by representatives elected by the people.

The United States, Mexico, France, Switzerland, and all South American nations are republics, and the republican principle of government is growing in popularity throughout the civilized world.

No form of government is equally good for all peoples. A certain form may be good for one country and bad for another country. A republic, which is the best government for a well-educated and virtuous people, is the worst for an ignorant and depraved people.

The excellence of a republican government depends upon the knowledge and virtue of its citizens. The people are the rulers, and, if they are wise and virtuous, they will rule well; if they are ignorant and depraved, they will rule ill. Therefore the hope of a republic like ours is, that its people will continue to grow wiser and better.

[1]Fiske's Civil Government of the United States.

SUGGESTIVE QUESTIONS.

1. Why is military government more severe than civil government?

2. Could society exist without law? Why?

3. Why is a republic a bad form of government for an ignorant people?

4. Are the people of the United States growing wiser and better?

5. Is this State improving in civilization?

## CHAPTER XVI.

## JUSTICE.

The object of government is to protect the people, and to render justice to them. Justice is the security of rights. A right is a well-founded claim; that is, a just claim of one person upon other persons.

Rights are the most important things that a person can possess, because his happiness depends upon them. They are real things, for whose protection governments are instituted. The kind and extent of the rights recognized and protected in any country determine the form of its government. As a rule, there is more freedom among citizens of a republic than among those of other governments, because a republic guarantees more rights.

### RIGHTS AND DUTIES.

People have many rights, and they have as many duties. Each right given to a person is a trust placed in his hands for him to discharge. A right implies a duty, and a duty implies a right. Rights and duties go hand in hand. For example, children have a right to the protection of their parents, and this implies that it is the duty of children to obey their parents.

CIVIL RIGHTS AND DUTIES.--Rights and duties are civil and political. Civil rights are sometimes called inalienable rights, because they can not be justly taken away except as a punishment for crime. They are chiefly those rights with which we are endowed by nature. They are not conferred by any earthly power, but are given to every human being at his birth. They are called civil rights, because they belong to the citizen in his ordinary daily life. Among civil rights are:

1. The right to personal security; that is, the right to be free from attack and annoyance;

2. The right of personal liberty; that is, to go when and where he pleases, provided he does not trespass upon the rights of others; and

3. The right of private property; that is, the right to use, enjoy, and dispose of what he has acquired by labor, purchase, gift, or inheritance.

The greater part of these rights belong to men whether living in society, that is, under government, or living without government. Their natural rights are more extensive without society than with it, but are far less secure. Without government natural rights are unlimited; each person may lay claim to all land and to all it produces, provided he is strong enough to maintain his claim by force.

When men join the social compact, they agree to abandon some of their natural rights, in order to be protected by the government in those which they retain; that is, each person agrees that in making his own claims he will have due regard for the similar claims of others.

In entering the social compact, men also agree to submit their personal claims to settlement by the law, instead of going to war to maintain them. They agree to refer their disputes to courts established for that purpose. As a rule, under government, right prevails; without government, might prevails.

Civil rights are divided into industrial rights, social rights, and moral or religious rights.

INDUSTRIAL RIGHTS AND DUTIES.--It is the right and duty of each person to provide in his own way, providing it is legal and honest, for himself and those dependent upon him. All business transactions; the search for homes, comforts, and wealth; agriculture, manufacturing, mining, and commerce; the conduct of all professions, occupations, and industries; the interests of farm laborers, operatives in factories, miners, clerks, and all persons engaged in mental or physical labor, are based upon industrial rights and duties.

The wages of people, the hours of labor, railway and telegraph lines, canals, express companies, other common carriers, the various kinds of employment, and the organization of men in different branches of industry to advance their interests, are questions affecting industrial rights. These rights underlie all efforts of people to improve their financial condition.

SOCIAL RIGHTS AND DUTIES.--Each member of society has rights as such, and these are called social rights. They include the rights of personal security and protection. They underlie all efforts for the improvement of the social condition of the people. Society is interested in better schools, in public health, in the reformation of criminals, in good highways and streets, in safe buildings, in well-lighted cities and villages, in the maintenance of charitable institutions, in the establishment of sources of harmless amusement, and in the preservation of peace and order.

The comfort and convenience of the public are even more important than the comfort and convenience of any person. Therefore, individual rights must yield to public rights when the two conflict. For example, the land of a private citizen may be condemned by the proper authorities, and be used for public highways or other public purposes. The government pays the owner of the property condemned, but usually less than his estimate of the value.

This right of society, existing above the right, of any of its members, is called the RIGHT OF EMINENT DOMAIN. By it individual rights must yield to the rights of society, of the government, or of a corporation. A corporation is an association of individuals authorized by law to transact business as a single natural person. Railway companies, banks, chartered cities and villages, and the counties of some States are corporations.

MORAL RIGHTS AND DUTIES.--Man is a moral being; that is, he is conscious of good and evil. Therefore he has moral rights and duties.

He has rights of conscience, with which it is not the province of government to interfere. He naturally worships a Being superior to himself, and feels the obligation to deal justly with his fellow-men. He has a right to do and say all things which are not unlawful or wrong within themselves. It is his right to worship when he pleases, whom he pleases, and as he pleases.

The moral rights and duties of the people are concerned in the maintenance of religion, the support of churches, in reverence for things sacred, in acts of charity and benevolence, in living an upright life, and in teaching lessons of morality, honesty, industry, and usefulness. Whatever is implied in the word ought, correctly used, is a moral duty.

POLITICAL RIGHTS AND DUTIES.--By the social compact, men also agree to abandon a part of their natural rights in order to participate in the government. They agree in part to be governed by others, in order that in part they may govern others. The rights of participation in the government, such as voting and holding office, are called political rights, because they affect the public policy of society.

Political rights do not belong to men by nature, but are conferred by government. Within reasonable bounds, they may be enlarged or restricted without injustice. Since they are conferred by the government, the power to vote and to hold office is a privilege to be enjoyed rather than a right to be asserted.

In the United States the political rights of the people are carefully set forth in the Constitution. The smallest functions of government, such as the size and color of a postage stamp, or the employment of a page in the State legislature, touch the political rights of the citizen. Appointment and elections to public office, the enactment of laws, and the performance of public duties are questions of political concern.

Good laws, good administrations, and the perpetuity of the government itself, depend upon the manner in which the people discharge their public duties. A man who habitually fails to vote and to take interest in the political affairs of his country may be a good man, but he is certainly a bad citizen.

To be a good citizen is to aid intelligently in giving the people good government. For a man to hold himself aloof from politics, unless his action is based upon conscientious scruples, shows his interest in himself, and his lack of interest in his country.

SUGGESTIVE QUESTIONS.

1. Why does happiness depend upon the maintenance of rights?

2. How do persons born under government agree to be governed by the laws?

3. If the claims of people as to their rights conflict, how is the difference settled?

4. What is meant by the phrase "common carrier"?

5. Is it right for men to hold aloof from public affairs because there is corruption in politics?

## CHAPTER XVII.

### LAW AND LIBERTY.

Through law rights are secured, and the performance of some duties is enforced. Law is a rule of action, prescribing what shall be done and what shall not be done. Laws exist for the purpose of securing the rights of the people. The enjoyment of rights is liberty.

As the enjoyment of rights depends upon their security, and as they are secured by law, therefore liberty is based upon law. Without law there could be no political liberty, and the civil liberty of the people would be narrow and uncertain. It may be said, therefore, that there can be no true liberty without law; but laws may be so many and so stringent that there can be no liberty. Liberty and just laws are inseparable.

Liberty and rights are of the same kinds, industrial, social, moral or religious, and political. The words "rights," "law," and "liberty" are full of meaning, and in a free country suggest ideas of the deepest reverence.

ORIGIN.--The laws of the country are partly human and partly divine. They were framed by man, but some of them are based upon the laws of God. Some are of recent origin, and many are so ancient that their beginning can not be traced. When men began, to live in society, they began to make laws, for laws at once became necessary. Laws are undergoing constant changes, as new conditions arise and new customs prevail.

## KINDS OF LAW.

The moral law prescribes our duties to men, and also to God. It is summed up and revealed in the Ten Commandments, and is the same as the law of nature taught us by our consciences.

The common law consists of the principles and rules of action applied by the courts in cases not regulated by express legislative acts. It is the unwritten law which has been practiced for ages in England and the United States. In all States of the Union, except Louisiana, cases not covered by the acts of the legislature are tried by the common law.

The civil law is the law that prevailed among the ancient Romans. It is still in use among most of the nations of continental Europe. In Louisiana it is applied to cases not covered by the laws of the legislature. The words civil law are sometimes used to denote the law governing civil suits.

Statute law consists of the acts passed by legislative assemblies. The words are used to denote the opposite of common law. The enactment of a statute by a State legislature repeals the common law previously in force upon the same subject.

International law, often called the law of nations, consists of the rules and customs prevailing between civilized nations in their relations with one another. It is based upon the law of nature, the law of right and wrong.

Criminal law is the law governing criminal cases. It is partly common law and partly statute law. "Ignorance of the law excuses no one."

Parliamentary law consists of the rules and customs governing parliamentary assemblies. It prevails in all law-making bodies, in conventions and deliberative meetings.

Martial law is the law which regulates men in military service. It prevails in the army and the navy. The courts which apply it are called courts martial. Martial law is noted for its severity.

Maritime law, or marine law, is the law especially relating to the business of the sea, to ships, their crews, and navigation. The courts of maritime law are admiralty courts.

Commercial law is a system of rules for the regulation of trade and commerce. It is deduced from the customs of merchants.

COURTS.--Laws are administered, that is, explained and applied, by means of courts. A court is a body organized for the public administration of justice. A court may consist of a single judge or justice, or of a number of judges acting together.

A court can administer the laws only in cases which are brought before it. The highest court in the land can not make an order or render a judgment until the question comes to trial in a regular way.

SUITS.--Suits at law are called causes, cases, or actions.

A civil cause is a suit between persons, brought to recover rights or to secure compensation for their infraction.

A criminal cause is a charge brought by a State or by the United States against a person for the commission of a crime.

The plaintiff is the person who brings the suit. The defendant is the person against whom the suit is brought.

In all criminal cases in State courts, the State is the plaintiff; in other words, society prosecutes the offender in the name of the State. In criminal cases in the United States courts, the United States is the plaintiff.

JUDGES.--The judge represents the majesty of the law, and is often called the court. He maintains the dignity of the trial, determines the method of procedure, interprets the law, instructs the juries, renders judgment, and in criminal cases passes sentence upon the offender. Judges are presumed to be learned in the law, and to be perfectly just and impartial in their rulings.

JURIES.--Most of the courts of this country have two juries, called respectively, grand jury and trial jury (or petit jury).

The purpose of the grand jury is to investigate crime, and to present charges, called indictments, for trial by the court. The number of grand jurors to the court varies in different States, being not more than twenty-four and not less than twelve. The grand jury has a foreman, elected by it, or appointed by the judge of the court.

The grand jury inquires into violations of the law, and if, in the judgment of twelve jurors, the evidence in a particular case warrants a trial, a formal written charge is prepared, and the foreman indorses thereon, "A true bill." Upon this indictment the offender is tried by the court.

In a few States grand juries are rarely if ever called, the indictment being found "on information" or on evidence presented to a court commissioner.

A trial jury usually consists of twelve men, but in some States a smaller number may be accepted by the judge of the court, in certain cases, by the agreement of the counsel upon the opposing sides. The trial jury hears the testimony and argument, and then decides upon the truth of the facts in dispute, and renders a verdict or decision in the suit, and in criminal cases convicts or acquits.

In some States all the jurors must agree, or there is no verdict. In other States the jury may render a verdict by the agreement of less than the whole number of jurors. Under certain regulations a party to a suit may challenge, that is, reject, a part or all of the jurors, and have others selected in their stead.

ORIGIN OF JURIES.--Grand juries and trial juries are of great antiquity. It is thought that they existed among the Saxons in the north of Europe before they invaded and settled England, more than fourteen hundred years ago. The jury system and many other political institutions of the United States are derived from England.

Both the grand jury and the trial jury are firmly grounded in this country, being recognized, in the constitutions of nearly all the States and the Constitution of the United States, and are regarded as among the strongest supports of a free government.

OFFICERS OF COURTS.--Each court has one or more ministerial officers, variously designated as constable, sheriff, tipstaff, or marshal. Each court also has one or more clerks, and sometimes other officers. Attorneys are considered officers of the courts in which they practice. They usually represent the plaintiff and the defendant in court and are then called counsel.

LEGAL PROCEEDINGS in civil cases begin by the court issuing a writ, at the instance of plaintiff, summoning defendant to appear. The defendant responding, pleadings are filed--the claims of plaintiff, and answer or demurrer of defendant. If these disagree as to facts, the court subpoenas witnesses. In the presence of judge and jury, the plaintiff states his case and the defendant his defense, witnesses are examined and cross-examined, and the case is argued. The judge then charges the jury--summarizing the evidence and indicating points to be decided; the jury retire to prepare their verdict, which is announced and recorded as the judgment of the court.

In criminal cases the accused may be arrested on a grand jury indictment or a magistrate's warrant. Unless the crime is murder, the accused may be released upon bail until trial, which proceeds as in civil cases.

SUGGESTIVE QUESTIONS.

1. Why does the State prosecute offenses, instead of leaving this duty to private persons?

2. What is meant by passing sentence upon an offender?

3. Do you believe in the jury system, or in the trial by several judges sitting together? Why?

4. Have you ever seen a court in session?

5. In this State a grand jury has how many members?

CHAPTER XVIII.

SUFFRAGE AND ELECTIONS.

SUFFRAGE.--The most important political right is the right of suffrage; that is, the right to vote. As the government exists for the benefit of the governed, the purpose of suffrage is to place it under their control. It gives each qualified voter a voice in public affairs, and places the country under the rule of the people.

As the interests of the voters and their families are the same, and as the voters represent these interests, the whole people, including women and children, have an influence in the government. The whole machinery of the State and of the United States is in the hands of those who do the voting.

IMPORTANCE.--The importance of this right can scarcely be overestimated. It constitutes the difference between a free country and a despotism. There can be no freedom unless the right to vote resides in the people; nor can there be good government unless this right is exercised with an intelligent regard for the public welfare. Yet vast numbers of voters never realize the power they wield or the great responsibility it entails upon them.

ELECTIONS.--The right of suffrage is exercised by means of elections. An election is the direct method of ascertaining the will of the people upon public affairs. They are held for the purpose of giving the people opportunity to express their choice in the selection of officers, and thus to make known their will upon questions of public concern.

METHODS OF VOTING.--There are three methods of voting--viva voce, by ballot, and by machine. A man votes viva voce by announcing to the election officers the name of the candidate of his choice, and having it recorded upon the polling-list. A man votes by ballot by handing to the officers a slip of paper containing the name of the candidate voted for. The officers deposit the ballots in a box called the ballot-box. A voting machine has a knob or lever for each candidate, and is so arranged that the voter can record one vote.

The viva voce method was once considered the best; but voting by ballot or by machine has supplanted it generally in the United States.

The Australian system provides at each polling-place a private apartment, called a booth, where each voter in private prepares his ballot from a printed list of all the candidates, and then hands it to the officers, who deposit it in the ballot-box.[1]

OFFICERS OF ELECTIONS.--The officers of elections at each polling-place are usually two or more supervisors, inspectors, or judges; a clerk; and a sheriff, marshal, or other officer of the peace.

The supervisors or inspectors decide who are entitled to vote under the law, and in elections by ballot they deposit the ballots in the ballot-box.

The clerk makes a list of the names of voters, and when the election is viva voce he records the votes.

The sheriff or other peace officer preserves order at the polls, has charge of the ballot-box and polling-list after the election closes, and delivers them to the proper authorities.

In most States, at the close of the election the officers canvass, that is, examine the votes cast, and certify the number of votes received by each candidate.

In some States the ballot-box is sealed at the close of the election, and delivered to the canvassing board of the county. In such cases the canvassing board of the county canvasses the vote, and in State and national elections sends returns to the canvassing board of the State at the State capital.

In some States election officers are appointed by the county officers, usually by the county judge or probate judge; in other States they are elected by the people.

BRIBERY.--Bribery in elections is one of the serious evils of politics. Bribery is offering or receiving a reward for voting. In most States, in addition to other penalties, persons convicted of giving or taking bribes are disfranchised; that is, are not permitted to vote thereafter. In ancient Athens a man convicted of corrupting a voter suffered the penalty of death.

The selling of a vote is regarded as one of the most infamous crimes that men can commit. Not even the conviction of theft so lowers a man in public esteem as a conviction of selling his vote, for bribery savors of both theft and treason.

To sell his suffrage is to sell his manhood, his country, and his convictions. Most men who sell their votes do it through ignorance; they are not aware of the enormity of the crime. He who knows its infamy, and yet barters his suffrage for money, is unworthy of the smallest trust, or even of the recognition of honest men.

[1]For details regarding this system see Chapter XIX.

SUGGESTIVE QUESTIONS.

1. In what way are voters responsible for the government of the country?

2. Do you believe in frequent elections? Why?

3. Do you believe in public voting or in secret voting? Why?

4. Why should election officers be fair and honest men?

5. What do you think of vote-buying and vote-selling?

CHAPTER XIX.

THE AUSTRALIAN BALLOT SYSTEM.

ORIGIN.--The idea of the secret ballot system, now known under its various modifications as the Australian Ballot System, was first proposed by Francis S. Dutton, member of the legislature of South Australia from 1851 to 1865. At that time the vices frequently accompanying open elections had begun to flourish in Australia. Bribery, intimidation, disorder, and violence were the order of all election days. The plan was elaborated, and became a law under the name of the "Elections Act" in 1857.

The beneficial results of this method soon became evident to other countries, and the movement spread to Europe, Canada, and the United States.

IN THE UNITED STATES.--A similar system to that originally adopted in Australia was first introduced into the United States by its adoption in 1888 in the State of Massachusetts and in the city of Louisville, Kentucky. The next year the legislatures of Indiana, Montana, Rhode Island, Wisconsin, Tennessee, Minnesota, Missouri, Michigan, and Connecticut passed laws providing for new systems of voting, more or less resembling the Australian system; and now their example has been followed by almost all the other States.

PRINCIPLES.--Although there are many modifications of detail in the statutes of the various States, there are two essential features of the ballot-reform system which are everywhere observed:

First, An arrangement of polling, by which compulsory secrecy of voting is secured, and intimidation or corruption of voters is prevented.

Second, One or more official ballots, printed and distributed under authority, on which the names of all candidates are found.

REQUIREMENTS.--The following are the requirements of the system: Ballots must be provided by public expense, and none but these ballots may be used. On these ballots should be printed the names of all candidates who have been nominated previously to the election, with the names of the offices for which they have been nominated and of the parties they represent.

There are two forms of ballots: the blanket ballot and the individual ballot. The former is arranged in some States so as to group candidates by parties, and in other States by the offices for which they are nominated. In many cases the names of candidates are alphabetically arranged, so that there can be no accusation of giving one party or candidate precedence as to position on the ticket. In a few cases, the name of the party to which the candidate belongs does not appear on the ballot at all, but only the name of the office for which he has been nominated; but in most cases the name of each party is printed either at the head of the ticket or opposite the name of each candidate, or in both places.

Where individual ballots are used, a separate ballot is printed for each party or independent ticket.

VOTING.--Special sworn clerks are engaged to distribute these ballots to voters at the polls.

The voter is allowed a limited time--say five or ten minutes--to retire into an election booth erected for the purpose, to make his choice of candidates or ballots. If the blanket ballot is in use, he does this by placing a cross opposite the name of the desired candidate or list of candidates; or by crossing out all others; or by means of pasters for the substitution of names. If individual ballots are provided, he selects the one he prefers, or corrects it to his liking by pasting upon it a single name or an entire ticket. If he prefers, he may write the names of candidates of his own nomination in place of those already printed. He, then, without communicating with any one, deposits his ballot as his vote. Only one man is allowed to enter a booth at a time, and none but the ballot clerks and the man about to deposit his ballot are allowed within the enclosure erected for the purpose.

In some States the booths are separated one from the other merely by partitions, as indicated in the cut, page 181; but in other States each booth is a separate compartment with a door, which is closed to prevent even a suspicion of any external observation.

In many States, assistance is rendered to the illiterate or the blind. In some cases, in order to aid those who can not read, each party adopts a device, as an eagle or a flag, which is printed on the ballot. In most States a voter who declares that he can not read, or that by some physical disability he is unable to mark his ballot, may receive the assistance of one or two of the election officers in marking it.

Every ballot must be strictly accounted for. If any person in preparing a ballot should spoil it, he may obtain others, one at a time, not exceeding three in all, provided he returns each spoiled one. All ballots thus returned are either immediately burned or else cancelled and preserved by the clerk.

ADVANTAGES.--The advantages which have already accrued from the adoption of these laws are manifold:

First, A secret ballot offers an effectual preventive against bribery, since no man will place his money corruptly without satisfying himself that the vote is placed according to agreement.

Second, It secures the voter against the coercion, solicitation, or intimidation of others, and enables him to vote according to the dictates of his conscience.

Third, Bargaining and trading at the polls is prevented, and with these much tumult, riot, and disorder must of necessity disappear.

Fourth, Money is made less of a factor in politics, and the poor man is placed on a plane of equality with the rich as a candidate.

In addition to these obvious advantages, the ballot reform movement promises to have much wider effects, and to pave the way and lay the foundation for other political reforms.

FORMS OF BALLOTS.--On pages 185, 186, and 187 are given forms of ballots and other matter illustrating various methods employed in carrying out the ballot laws of the States. It will be observed that each of these three ballots is representative of a different method.

In the first ballot shown, no party name appears, and the names of candidates for each office are arranged in alphabetical order. On this form of ballot, which most resembles that used in Australia, the individual candidate is made prominent, and party connection does not appear at all.

Second, In the Massachusetts ballot, the names of the candidates are arranged alphabetically under each office, but in addition to this, the party name appears opposite the name of each candidate. On this form of ballot, while the party connection of each candidate is indicated, greater prominence is given to the individual, and the voter is required to make choice of a candidate for each office separately. He cannot vote a straight ticket by a single mark.

Third, In the Indiana ticket, the names are grouped according to party, not according to office, the party name appearing at the head of the ballot as well as at the side of each name. On this form of ballot, the party connection of the candidate is made most prominent, and while provision is made for voting for individuals representing different parties, still the voting of a straight ticket is made most easy.

Many States use the party-column principle of the Indiana ticket, but modify the form of the ticket in various details. The party emblem is sometimes omitted from the circle used in voting a straight picket, or placed just above that circle. The square opposite each candidate's name is sometimes placed after the name instead of before it; and is usually left blank.

A fourth form, namely, that of the individual ballot as used in the State of New Jersey, can not be here shown, as a separate ballot is required for each party or each independent nomination. These separate ballots are all official, and are furnished at public expense; but the use of an unofficial ballot is practically allowed, since the voter is permitted to take to the voting booth a paster ballot containing a complete party ticket, printed and furnished at party expense. This he can paste over the official ballot and deposit as his vote.

SUGGESTIVE QUESTIONS.

1. What is meant by the Australian ballot system?

2. Name some places in the United States in which a similar system of reform has been adopted.

3. What are the essential principles of the system?

4. What are the necessary requirements for carrying out the law?

5. What is the object in providing official ballots?

6. Describe two kinds of polling booths used.

7. What are the obvious advantages of the reform?

8. Describe the characteristic forms of ballot used in various States which have adopted the reform.

9. Mention the advantages and the disadvantages of the city ballot shown on page 185.

10. Compare the Massachusetts ballot with the Indiana ballot, and note their differences.

Which system of voting is likely to secure the best public officers: that represented in the city ballot of 1890, in the Massachusetts ballot, or in the Indiana ballot?

CHAPTER XX.

PARTIES AND PARTY MACHINERY.

Wherever the right to vote exists, the people naturally form themselves into political parties.

A political party is an organization of voters maintained for the purpose of impressing its principles upon the public policy of the country. Men have divers views as to the duties, scope, and proper measures of the government, and these divers views lead to the formation of opposing parties. In a free country the majority must rule, and parties are the means by which majorities are ascertained.

ORIGIN.--Parties usually grow out of questions of legislation, rather than out of questions of executive management or judicial interpretation. In other words, a party is formed to influence the passage of laws, rather than their execution or their application by the courts. But, when parties are once formed, they usually extend their influence to the selection of officers of all grades and all departments, even the least important officials of a township or civil district.

The presidential election has come to be the most exciting and bitter of all political contests, because of the large influence which the President exerts upon national legislation, and because of the immense patronage of his office.

NECESSITY.--Parties appear to be a necessity in all free governments. They serve as check upon one another, as the party in power is responsible for the public policy of the country. If the people are dissatisfied with the party in power, they can displace it and elect another in its stead. Parties are therefore placed upon their good behavior, and made to feel their responsibility to the people.

If there were no party organizations, many of the views of a candidate would not be known, and there could be no assurance that he would be true to the interests of the majority electing him. The fact that a public man is a member of a certain party shows many of the views which he entertains and the principles which he may be expected to support.

Party government is often bad, but as the party is responsible for the conduct of all officers elected by it, party government, especially in legislative affairs, is better than personal government, in which no one but the officer himself is responsible for his official conduct.

PARTY MACHINERY.--The machinery of parties in this country is very complex, and is closely interwoven with our system of government. Each party must select candidates for the various offices in the gift of the people, in order that it may exert its greatest power in elections and in public affairs. The people in each party must have a voice in the selection of candidates for township offices, district offices, county offices, State offices, and President and Vice President of the United States. Therefore each party has a system of committees, conventions, primary elections, and caucuses, for ascertaining the choice of its members for these various offices.

Parties and party machinery are not generally provided for in the law, but they exist by a custom almost as old as the government, and are firmly fixed in our political system.

COMMITTEES.--Each of the great parties has a national committee, consisting of one member from each State and Territory, chosen by its national convention. The national committee is the chief executive authority of the party. It calls the national convention, fixes the time and place for holding it, and the representation to which each State and Territory is entitled. It appoints a sub-committee of its members, called the campaign or executive committee, which conducts the political canvass or campaign, for the party.

The campaign committee distributes pamphlets, speeches, newspapers, and other political documents among the voters of the country; selects public speakers; makes appointments for them to speak; arranges for party meetings; collects funds to bear the expenses of the campaign, and has a general oversight of the party work in all the States.

Each party also has a State committee in each State, usually consisting of a member from each congressional district, in some States consisting of a member from each county; a district committee in each congressional, judicial, senatorial, and representative district, consisting of a member from each county composing the district; a county committee, consisting of a member from each township or civil district; and in some States, various other committees.

Each of these committees performs for the division for which it is selected duties similar to those which the national committee performs for the whole Union.

CONVENTIONS.--The method of ascertaining the choice of a party in the selection of candidates is either by a primary election or by a convention.

A political convention is an assemblage of the voters of a party, either in person or by representatives called delegates. If the voters assemble in person, the convention is called a primary or mass meeting.

The purpose of a convention may be to select candidates for office, to send delegates to a higher convention, to adopt a declaration of principles, or to decide upon a party policy. It is common for two or more of these purposes to come before the same convention.

CALLING CONVENTIONS.--In the year of the presidential election, the national committee calls a national convention, naming the time and place, and the representation of each State. The State committee calls a State convention to send delegates to the national convention; and, if a State election is approaching, it may direct that the convention shall also select candidates for State offices. In response to this call, the county committees order county conventions in all the counties of the State to send delegates to the State convention, and perhaps to select candidates for county offices. In some States the township committees order township conventions in all townships for the purpose of sending delegates to the county conventions, and perhaps to name candidates for township offices.

It will be seen that the calling of the various conventions connected directly or indirectly with the selection of candidates for President and Vice President proceeds from the highest downward. The same order is observed in other conventions, the call always beginning with the highest committee concerned and proceeding to the lowest.

LOCAL AND STATE CONVENTIONS.--The order of holding a system of conventions, however, proceeds from the lowest to the highest. The township holds a convention and sends delegates to the county convention. The county convention sends delegates to the State convention, and the State convention sends delegates to the national convention.

DELEGATES CHOSEN BY PRIMARIES.--In many states the delegates to all conventions are elected by the members of the party at primary elections. In some states even the delegates to the national convention are chosen in this manner.

NATIONAL CONVENTION.--A national convention is an important assemblage. It contains many distinguished men, and exerts great influence on the history of the country. A national convention usually consists of more than a thousand delegates. In a Democratic convention, for instance, there are four delegates from each State, two from each congressional district, and a few from the Territories.

In the selection of delegates to the national convention, the State convention often selects four, representing the two United States senators, and the members of the convention from each congressional district select two, representing the lower house of Congress. For each delegate the State convention also selects an alternate delegate, who attends the national convention in case the regular delegate can not be present.

The national convention is called to order by the chairman of the national committee. It then elects a temporary chairman, and afterward a permanent president. The convention appoints the national committee, calling upon the delegation from each State to name its member; adopts a declaration of principles, called a platform, for the approaching campaign; nominates candidates for President and Vice President, and performs various other work connected with the party organization.

PLATFORM.--The declaration of party principles adopted and issued by a convention is called a platform, and each separate statement of a principle is popularly called a plank.

The platform is an announcement of the policy to be pursued by the party if its candidates are elected, and is presumed to contain all the important principles upon which the voters of the party are agreed. Upon these principles the party claims the right to administer the public affairs of the country.

The platforms of State and local conventions are usually based upon the national platform of the same party, but also contain statements of principles upon local questions.

NOMINATIONS.--To nominate a candidate is to name him for office; that is, to place his name before the public. The person nominated is called the nominee, and all the nominees for a certain election constitute a ticket.

A nomination usually secures to a candidate the general support of the party. Voters may vote for other persons than the nominees, but the great body of voters usually support the tickets of their respective parties. Nomination serves to prevent a great number of candidates, and thus simplifies the election.

PRIMARY ELECTIONS.--Candidates for township, county, and other offices are frequently chosen by means of primary elections.

A primary election is an election in which the members of a party choose their candidates for office. As a rule, none but the members of the party holding it can vote in a primary election. Many persons prefer the primary, to a convention, believing the former to be a fairer and more impartial method of ascertaining the choice of the party. The voting is usually by ballot.

In many States primary elections are under the control of the law, and are guarded by the same restrictions that pertain to other elections.

CAUCUSES.--A meeting composed of the members of a legislative body who are of the same party, and assembled for party purposes, is called a caucus. Ward conventions in cities are sometimes called by the same name.

The usual purpose of a caucus is to nominate candidates for offices within the gift of the legislative body, or to consider questions of legislation. A caucus elects a chairman and other officers, but rarely if ever adopts a platform of principles. The great political parties of the country have caucuses in each branch of Congress, and usually in the legislatures of the several States.

SUGGESTIVE QUESTIONS.

1. Name the great parties that have existed in the United States.

2. Who are the respective chairmen of the national executive committees of the two great parties?

3. Read the last national platforms of the two great parties.

4. Which do you like better, primary elections or conventions? Why?

5. Should a member of a legislative body be influenced in his vote by the decision of the caucus of his party?

CHAPTER XXI.

LEGISLATION.

Legislation, the act or process of making laws, is the most important function of government. It is the most important, because it is the first step, and the enforcement and interpretation of laws depend upon their enactment. The laws of a country should be as few in number, as simple in construction, and as uniform in their application, as will meet the needs of the people. It is a great misfortune for the laws to bear unequally upon the people; to grant special privileges to one class, or to impose special hardships upon another class.

The great variety and volume of laws made by the national and the State legislatures of the United States have led to a close study of legislation. In no other country is the process of making laws so thoroughly mastered, or parliamentary law so generally understood.

BILLS.--The process of enacting a law, from its introduction to its final approval, is an intricate and interesting study. Until its passage and final approval, a measure is called either a bill or a resolution.

Bills and resolutions are very similar, the latter usually being simpler, and beginning with the words, "Be it resolved" or simply "Resolved," while the former begin with the words, "Be it enacted." A joint resolution as well as a bill requires the concurrence of both houses of a legislative assembly to make it a law.

INTRODUCTION.--The introduction of a bill is the first presentation of it to a legislative body for action. This is usually done by asking "leave" of the body, either orally or in writing, to bring the measure before it. This leave to present is rarely if ever refused.

The rules require that after its introduction it shall be three times read aloud before its passage. These three readings do not refer to readings for information as to its provisions. The constitutions of nearly all States require that the three readings shall be on three different days; but in most of them this rule, may be suspended by a two thirds, three fourths, four fifths, or unanimous vote, the requisite majority varying in different States.

COMMITTEES.--When a bill or resolution is introduced, it is usual to refer it to a committee for a critical consideration. A committee usually consists of from three to thirteen members, of whom the first named is usually chairman, presumably selected for their knowledge of the subjects to come before them.

A standing committee lasts during the entire session. Most legislative bodies have from twenty to forty standing committees.

A special or select committee is raised for a special purpose, and is usually adjourned when its report is made.

A committee of the whole consists of all the members of a body sitting as a committee. In committees of the whole the regular presiding officer usually vacates the chair, calling some other member of the body to act as chairman. The principal part of the work of a legislative body is perfected by its committees. They discuss the merits and demerits of bills, and perfect such as, in their judgment, should pass.

REPORTS.--The committee to whom a bill has been referred critically examines it, and usually reports it to the body, either favorably or unfavorably, recommending that it should pass or should not pass. If the members of a committee are equally or nearly equally divided as to the merits of the bill, it may be reported without an expression of opinion.

When important bills are reported by a committee they are usually discussed by the members of the body. The debate on the measure usually brings out the reasons for, and those against, its passage. Many bills are several times recommitted--that is, again referred to a committee--before their passage.

In some legislative bodies, especially in the Congress of the United States, a great many bills are pigeon-holed by committees; that is, are filed away and never reported. The reports of the committees, whether favorable or unfavorable, are usually adopted by the body, and therefore have an important bearing upon legislation.

AMENDMENTS.--In most legislative bodies a bill may be amended at the pleasure of the majority, before it is read the third time. Amendments are made for the purpose of perfecting the measure. A bill may be amended by striking out some of its provisions, by striking out and inserting, or by inserting.

A bill passed by one house of a legislature maybe amended by the other house, but, if amended, must be returned with the amendment to the house in which it originated, in order that the amendment may be considered. If one house amends and the other refuses to accept, the bill is often referred to a conference committee of members of both houses. If this does not secure agreement, and both adhere to their original action, the bill fails.

PASSAGE.--When a bill passes the house in which it originated, the clerk transmits and reports it to the other house for action. The house to which it is transmitted may pass it without commitment, but usually refers it to a committee, and, when reported, may pass it or reject it, or amend it and return it with the amendment to the house in which it originated.

When passed by both houses, the bill is engrossed--that is, rewritten without blots or erasures--and transmitted to the President or governor, as the case may be, for his approval. If approved and signed, or if not returned within a fixed time, the bill becomes a law. If vetoed, it must be again considered by both bodies, and is lost unless again passed by each, and in Congress and in many States by a two thirds vote.

## SUGGESTIVE QUESTIONS.

1. Obtain from any convenient source and present in the recitation a sample of a bill, and also of a resolution.

2. Why should a bill have three separate readings on three different days?

3. Why is the report of a committee generally adopted by the body?

4. Why are chairmanships of committees usually much sought after in legislative bodies?

5. Present in the recitation a copy of the report of a legislative committee upon some subject.

## CHAPTER XXII.

## REVENUE AND TAXATION.

Revenue.--The regulation of revenue and taxation is one of the most important and difficult questions of government. One of the wisest of modern statesmen has said that the management of finance is government.

Government, whatever its form, is an intricate and expensive machine, and therefore sure and ample sources of revenue are as necessary to it as blood is to the human body. The necessary expenses of a local community, such as a village, a city, or a county, are heavy; while those of a State are immense, and those of a nation almost beyond conception. These expenses must be promptly met, or the government becomes bankrupt, lacking in respect, without power to enforce its rights even among its own people, and finally ceases to exist.

TAXATION.--The chief source of revenue in all governments is taxation. A tax is a portion of private property taken by the government for public purposes. Taxation, the act of laying taxes, is regarded as the highest function of government. It is also one of the most delicate, because it touches the people directly, and is therefore frequently the cause of discontent among the masses.

The government makes no direct return to the citizen for the taxes it exacts, and in this respect only does taxation differ from the exercise of the right of eminent domain. How much revenue must be raised? what articles should be taxed? what should be the rate of taxation? are questions that concern every government.

As a person may be at the same time a citizen of a village, a township, a county, a State, and the United States, so he may, during the same year, pay a separate tax to each of these five governments.

NECESSITY OF TAXATION.--Taxation is one of the necessary burdens of society. A government as well as an individual must have money to pay its expenses, and the principal part, if not all, of this money must be raised by taxation of one kind or another. Men may differ as to the kind and the rate of taxation, but taxes must be paid in order that government may exist. The tax payer receives no immediate return for his taxes, but has a constant return in the way of protection to life, liberty, and property, the enjoyment of public conveniences, and the improvement of society.

By means of taxes each person bears his part in the cost of maintaining the social compact. He gives up a portion of his property in order that what remains may be the more secure and valuable, and that he may enjoy many other blessings that would otherwise be impossible. Although the rate is often high, even higher than necessary, it is safe to say that every tax payer of the country receives from the government more than he contributes by taxation.

Taxes are direct or indirect.

DIRECT TAXES.--A direct tax is levied directly at a given rate upon property or polls. Taxes levied by villages, towns, townships, cities, counties, and States are for the most part direct taxes.

A poll tax is levied upon the polls, or heads, of the male inhabitants who have attained a certain age, usually twenty-one years.

A property tax, as the name indicates, is levied upon property. Property is of two kinds, real and personal.

Real property, usually called real estate, consists of lands and buildings.

Personal property is that which can be moved from place to place, and includes everything that a person can own except real estate.

In all systems of taxation, much real estate, such as churches, cemeteries, colleges, charitable institutions, and public buildings, is exempt from taxes.

Five times in its history--namely, in 1798, 1813, 1815, 1816, and 1861--the United States levied a direct tax upon the people, but in each case the law was in force but a single year. From 1861 to 1871 there was also an income tax; that is, a tax of a given per cent. upon all annual incomes that exceeded a certain amount. In 1913, Congress passed a new income tax law, with additional taxes on very large incomes.

INDIRECT TAXES.--An indirect tax is assessed upon the property of one person, but is indirectly paid by another. The owner of the property at the time of assessment pays the tax to the government, but a part or all of the tax is ultimately paid by the consumer of the goods. All taxes now levied by the national government are indirect.

The indirect taxes levied by the national government are customs, or duties, and internal revenue.

CUSTOMS, OR DUTIES.--Customs, or duties, are taxes levied upon certain goods imported from foreign countries. The Constitution prohibits the taxation of exports.

The schedule or list of articles taxed and of duties to be paid is called the tariff. Custom dues are collected by officers of the national government at the custom-houses, located at the ports of entry, usually, but not always, on or near the sea-coast. By far the larger portion of the national revenue is derived from customs.

INTERNAL REVENUE.--Internal revenue, sometimes called excise, is a tax levied upon certain articles produced in this country, such as tobacco and spirituous liquors. It is collected by officers of the national government, called collectors, stationed in different parts of the country.

SUGGESTIVE QUESTIONS.

1. Name some of the items of expense in village government.

2. In township government.

3. In city government.

4. In county government.

5. In State government.

6. In national government.

7. What is the rate of property taxation in this country?

8. What is the rate in this State?

9. Where is the nearest custom-house?

## CONSTITUTION OF THE UNITED STATES.

### PREAMBLE.

We, the people of the United States, in order to form a more perfect union, establish justice, insure domestic tranquillity, provide for the common defense, promote the general welfare, and secure the blessings of liberty to ourselves and our posterity, do ordain and establish this Constitution for the United States of America.

### ARTICLE I. LEGISLATIVE DEPARTMENT.

SECTION I. Congress in General.

All legislative powers herein granted shall be vested in a Congress of the United States, which shall consist of a Senate and House of Representatives.

SECTION II. House of Representatives.

Clause 1. The House of Representatives shall be composed of members chosen every second year by the people of the several states; and the electors in each state shall have the qualifications requisite for electors of the most numerous branch of the State Legislature.

Clause 2. No person shall be a representative who shall not have attained to the age of twenty-five years, and been seven years a citizen of the United States, and who shall not, when elected, be an inhabitant of that state in which he shall be chosen.

Clause 3. Representatives and direct taxes shall be apportioned among the several states which may be included within this Union, according to their respective numbers, which shall be determined by adding to the whole number of free persons, including those bound to service for a term of years, and excluding Indians not taxed, three-fifths of all other persons. The actual enumeration shall be made within three years after the first meeting of the Congress of the United States, and within every subsequent term of ten years, in such manner as they shall by law direct. The number of representatives shall not exceed one for every thirty thousand, but each state shall have at least one representative; and until such enumeration shall be made, the state of New Hampshire shall be entitled to choose three, Massachusetts eight, Rhode Island and Providence Plantations one, Connecticut five, New York six, New Jersey four, Pennsylvania eight, Delaware one, Maryland six, Virginia ten, North Carolina five, South Carolina five, and Georgia three.

Clause 4. When vacancies happen in the representation from any state, the executive authority thereof shall issue writs of election to fill such vacancies.

Clause 5. The House of Representatives shall choose their speaker and other officers, and shall have the sole power of impeachment.

SECTION III. Senate.

Clause 1. The Senate of the United States shall be composed of two senators from each state, chosen by the [Legislature][1] thereof for six years, and each senator shall have one vote.

Clause 2. Immediately after they shall be assembled in consequence of the first election, they shall be divided, as equally as may be, into three classes. The seats of the senators of the first class shall be vacated at the expiration of the second year, of the second class at the expiration of the fourth year, and of the third class at the expiration of the sixth year, so that one-third may be chosen every second year; [and if vacancies happen, by resignation or otherwise, during the recess of the Legislature of any state, the executive thereof may make temporary appointments until the next meeting of the Legislature, which shall then fill such vacancies.][1]

Clause 3. No person shall be a senator who shall not have attained to the age of thirty years, and been nine years a citizen of the United States, and who shall not, when elected, be an inhabitant of that state for which he shall be chosen.

Clause 4. The Vice-president of the United States shall be President of the Senate, but shall have no vote, unless they be equally divided.

Clause 5. The Senate shall choose their other officers, and also a president pro tempore, in the absence of the Vice-president, or when he shall exercise the office of President of the United States.

Clause 6. The Senate shall have the sole power to try all impeachments. When sitting for that purpose, they shall be on oath or affirmation. When the President of the United States is tried, the chief justice shall preside; and no person shall be convicted without the concurrence of two-thirds of the members present.

Clause 7. Judgment in cases of impeachment shall not extend further than to removal from office, and disqualification to hold and enjoy any office of honor, trust, or profit under the United States; but the party convicted shall, nevertheless, be liable and subject to indictment, trial, judgment, and punishment according to law.

SECTION IV. Both Houses.

Clause 1. The times, places, and manner of holding elections for senators and representatives shall be prescribed in each state by the Legislature thereof; but the Congress may at any time, by law, make or alter such regulations, except as to the places of choosing senators.

Clause 2. The Congress shall assemble at least once in every year, and such meeting shall be on the first Monday in December, unless they shall by law appoint a different day.

SECTION V. The Houses separately.

Clause 1. Each house shall be the judge of the elections, returns, and qualifications of its own members, and a majority of each shall constitute a quorum to do business; but a smaller number may adjourn from day to day, and may be authorized to compel the attendance of absent members, in such manner and under such penalties as each house may provide.

Clause 2. Each house may determine the rules of its proceedings, punish its members for disorderly behavior, and, with the concurrence of two-thirds, expel a member.

Clause 3. Each house shall keep a journal of its proceedings, and from time to time publish the same, excepting such parts as may in their judgment require secrecy; and the yeas and nays of the members of either house, on any question, shall, at the desire of one-fifth of those present, be entered on the journal.

Clause 4. Neither house during the session of Congress shall, without the consent of the other, adjourn for more than three days, nor to any other place than that in which the two houses shall be sitting.

SECTION VI. Disabilities of Members.

Clause 1. The senators and representatives shall receive a compensation for their services, to be ascertained by law, and paid out of the treasury of the United States. They shall in all cases, except treason, felony, and breach of the peace, be privileged from arrest during their attendance at the session of their respective houses, and in going to and returning from the same; and for any speech or debate in either house, they shall not be questioned in any other place.

Clause 2. No senator or representative shall, during the time for which he was elected, be appointed to any civil office under the authority of the United States, which shall have been created, or the emoluments whereof shall have been increased, during such time; and no person holding any office under the United States shall be a member of either house during his continuance in office.

SECTION VII. Mode of passing Laws.

Clause 1. All bills for raising revenue shall originate in the House of Representatives; but the Senate may propose or concur with amendments, as on other bills.

Clause 2. Every bill which shall have passed the House of Representatives and the Senate shall, before it become a law, be presented to the President of the United States; if he approve, he shall sign it; but if not, he shall return it, with his objections, to that house in which it shall have originated, who shall enter the objections at large on their journal, and proceed to reconsider it. If, after such reconsideration two-thirds of that house shall agree to pass the bill, it shall be sent, together with the objections, to the other house, by which it shall likewise be reconsidered, and if approved by two-thirds of that house, it shall become a law. But in all such cases the votes of both houses shall be determined by yeas and nays, and the names of the persons voting for and against the bill shall be entered on the journal of each house respectively. If any bill shall not be returned by the President within ten days (Sundays excepted) after it shall have been presented to him, the same shall be a law in like manner as if he had signed it, unless the Congress by their adjournment prevent its return, in which case it shall not be a law.

Clause 3. Every order, resolution, or vote to which the concurrence of the Senate and House of Representatives may be necessary (except on a question of adjournment) shall be presented to the President of the United States; and before the same shall take effect, shall be approved by him, or, being disapproved by him, shall be repassed by two-thirds of the Senate and House of Representatives, according to the rules and limitations prescribed in the case of a bill.

SECTION VIII. Powers granted to Congress.

The Congress shall have power--

Clause 1. To lay and collect taxes, duties, imposts, and excises, to pay the debts and provide for the common defense and general welfare of the United States; but all duties, imposts and excises shall be uniform throughout the United States;

Clause 2. To borrow money on the credit of the United States;

Clause 3. To regulate commerce with foreign nations, and among the several states, and with the Indian tribes;

Clause 4. To establish a uniform rule of naturalization and uniform laws on the subject of bankruptcies, throughout the United States;

Clause 5. To coin money, regulate the value thereof and of foreign coin, and fix the standard of weights and measures;

Clause 6. To provide for the punishment of counterfeiting the securities and current coin of the United States;

Clause 7. To establish post-offices and post-roads;

Clause 8. To promote the progress of science and useful arts, by securing for limited times to authors and inventors the exclusive right to their respective writings and discoveries;

Clause 9. To constitute tribunals inferior to the Supreme Court;

Clause 10. To define and punish piracies and felonies committed on the high seas, and offenses against the law of nations;

Clause 11. To declare war, grant letters of marque and reprisal, and make rules concerning captures on land and water;

Clause 12. To raise and support armies; but no appropriation of money to that use shall be for a longer term than two years;

Clause 13. To provide and maintain a navy;

Clause 14. To make rules for the government and regulation of the land and naval forces;

Clause 15. To provide for calling forth the militia to execute the laws of the Union, suppress insurrections, and repel invasions;

Clause 16. To provide for organizing, arming, and disciplining the militia, and for governing such part of them as may be employed in the service of the United States, reserving to the states respectively the appointment of the officers and the authority of training the militia according to the discipline prescribed by Congress;

Clause 17. To exercise exclusive legislation, in all cases whatsoever, over such district (not exceeding ten miles square) as may, by cession of particular states and the acceptance of Congress, become the seat of the government of the United States, and to exercise like authority over all places purchased, by the consent of the Legislature of the State in which the same shall be, for the erection of forts, magazines, arsenals, dock-yards, and other needful buildings; and

Clause 18. To make all laws which shall be necessary and proper for carrying into execution the foregoing powers, and all other powers vested by this Constitution in the government of the United Stales, or in any department or officer thereof,

SECTION IX. Powers denied to the United States.

Clause 1. The migration or importation of such persons as any of the states now existing shall think proper to admit, shall not be prohibited by the Congress prior to the year one thousand eight hundred and eight; but a tax or duty may be imposed on such importation, not exceeding ten dollars for each person.

Clause 2. The privilege of the writ of habeas corpus shall not be suspended unless when, in cases of rebellion or invasion, the public safety may require it.

Clause 3. No bill of attainder, or ex-post-facto law, shall he passed.

Clause 4. No capitation or other direct tax shall be laid, unless in proportion to the census or enumeration herein before directed to be taken.

Clause 5. No tax or duty shall be laid on articles exported from any state.

Clause 6. No preference shall be given by any regulation of commerce or revenue to the ports of one state over those of another; nor shall vessels bound to or from one state be obliged to enter, clear, or pay duties in another.

Clause 7. No money shall be drawn from the treasury but in consequence of appropriations made by law; and a regular statement and account of the receipts and expenditures of all public money shall be published from time to time.

Clause 8. No title of nobility shall be granted by the United States; and no person holding any office of profit or trust under them shall, without the consent of the Congress, accept of any present, emolument, office, or title of any kind whatever, from any king, prince, or foreign state.

SECTION X. Powers denied to the States.

Clause 1. No state shall enter into any treaty, alliance, or confederation; grant letters of marque and reprisal; coin money; emit bills of credit; make any thing but gold and silver coin a tender in payment of debts; pass any bill of attainder, ex-post-facto law, or law impairing the obligation of contracts; or grant any title of nobility.

Clause 2. No state shall, without the consent of the Congress, lay any imposts or duties on imports or exports except what may be absolutely necessary for executing its inspection laws; and the net produce of all duties and imposts laid by any state on imports or exports shall be for the use of the treasury of the United Stales; and all such laws shall be subject to the revision and control of the Congress.

Clause 3. No state shall, without the consent of Congress, lay any duty of tonnage, keep troops or ships of war in time of peace, enter into any agreement or compact with another state or with a foreign power, or engage in war, unless actually invaded, or in such imminent danger as will not admit of delay.

ARTICLE II. EXECUTIVE DEPARTMENT.

SECTION I. President and Vice-president.

Clause 1. The executive power shall be vested in a President of the United States of America. He shall hold his office during the term of four years, and, together with the Vice-president; chosen for the same term, be elected as follows:

Clause 2. Each state shall appoint, in such manner as the Legislature thereof may direct, a number of electors, equal to the whole number of senators and representatives to which the state may be entitled in the Congress; but no senator or representative, or person holding an office of trust or profit under the United States, shall be appointed an elector.

[Clause 3. The electors shall meet in their respective states, and vote by ballot for two persons, of whom one at least shall not be an inhabitant of the same state with themselves. And they shall make a list of all the persons voted for, and of the number of votes for each; which list they shall sign and certify, and transmit, sealed, to the seat of the government of the United States, directed to the President of the Senate. The President of the Senate shall, in the presence of the Senate and House of Representatives, open all the certificates, and the votes shall then be counted. The person having the greatest number of votes shall be the President, if such number be a majority of the whole number of electors appointed; and if there be more than one who have such majority, and have an equal number of votes, then the House of Representatives shall immediately choose by ballot one of them for President; and if no person have a majority, then, from the five highest on the list, the said House shall in like manner choose the President. But in choosing the President, the votes shall be taken by states, the representation from each state having one vote, a quorum for this purpose shall consist of a member or members from two-thirds of the states, and a majority of all the states shall be necessary to a choice. In every case, after the choice of the President, the person having the greatest number of votes of the electors shall be the Vice-president. But if there should remain two or more who have equal votes, the Senate shall choose from them by ballot the Vice-president.][2]

Clause 4. The Congress may determine the time of choosing the electors, and the day on which they shall give their votes, which day shall be the same throughout the United States.

Clause 5. No person except a natural-born citizen, or a citizen of the United States at the time of the adoption of this Constitution, shall be eligible to the office of President; neither shall any person be eligible to that office who shall not have attained to the age of thirty-five years, and been fourteen years a resident within the United States.

Clause 6. In case of the removal of the President from office, or of his death, resignation, or inability to discharge the powers and duties of the said office, the same shall devolve on the Vice-president; and the Congress may by law provide for the case of removal, death, resignation, or inability, both of the President and Vice-president, declaring what officer shall then act as President; and such officer shall act accordingly, until the disability be removed, or a President shall be elected.

Clause 7. The President shall, at stated times, receive for his services a compensation, which shall neither be increased nor diminished during the period for which he shall have been elected, and he shall not receive within that period any other emolument from the United States, or any of them.

Clause 8. Before he enter on the execution of his office, he shall take the following oath or affirmation:

"I do solemnly swear (or affirm) that I will faithfully execute the office of President of the United States, and will, to the best of my ability, preserve, protect, and defend the Constitution of the United States."

SECTION II. Powers of the President.

Clause 1. The President shall be commander-in-chief of the army and navy of the United States and of the militia of the several states, when called into the actual service of the United States; he may require the opinion in writing of the principal officer in each of the executive departments, upon any subject relating to the duties of their respective offices; and he shall have power to grant reprieves and pardons for offenses against the United States, except in cases of impeachment.

Clause 2. He shall have power, by and with the advice and consent of the Senate, to make treaties, provided two-thirds of the senators present concur; and he shall nominate, and by and with the advice and consent of the Senate shall appoint ambassadors, other public ministers and consuls, judges of the Supreme Court, and all other officers of the United States, whose appointments are not herein otherwise provided for, and which shall be established by law; but the Congress may by law vest the appointment of such inferior officers as they think proper in the President alone, in the courts of law, or in the heads of departments.

Clause 3. The President shall have power to fill up all vacancies that may happen during the recess of the Senate, by granting commissions, which shall expire at the end of their next session.

SECTION III. Duties of the President.

He shall, from time to time, give to the Congress information of the state of the Union, and recommend to their consideration such measures as he shall judge necessary and expedient; he may, on extraordinary occasions, convene both houses, or either of them; and in case of disagreement between them, with respect to the time of adjournment, he may adjourn them to such time as he shall think proper; he shall receive ambassadors and other public ministers; he shall take care that the laws be faithfully executed, and shall commission all the officers of the United States.

SECTION IV. Impeachment of the President.

The President, Vice-president, and all civil officers of the United States, shall be removed from office on impeachment for and conviction of treason, bribery, or other high crimes and misdemeanors.

## ARTICLE III. JUDICIAL DEPARTMENT.

### SECTION I. United States Courts.

The judicial power of the United States shall be vested in one Supreme Court, and in such inferior courts as the Congress may from time to time ordain and establish. The judges, both of the supreme and inferior courts, shall hold their offices during good behavior; and shall, at stated times, receive for their services a compensation, which shall not be diminished during their continuance in office.

### SECTION II. Jurisdiction of the United States Courts.

Clause 1. The judicial power shall extend to all cases in law and equity arising under this Constitution, the laws of the United States, and treaties made, or which shall be made, under their authority; to all cases affecting ambassadors, other public ministers, and consuls; to all cases of admiralty and maritime jurisdiction; to controversies to which the United States shall be a party; to controversies between two or more states; between a state and citizens of another state; between citizens of different states; between citizens of the same state claiming lands under grants of different states; and between a state, or the citizens thereof, and foreign states, citizens, or subjects.[3]

Clause 2. In all cases affecting ambassadors, other public ministers and consuls, and those in which a state shall be party, the Supreme Court, shall have original jurisdiction. In all the other cases before mentioned, the Supreme Court shall have appellate jurisdiction, both as to law and fact, with such exceptions, and under such regulations as the Congress shall make.

Clause 3. The trial of all crimes, except in cases of impeachment, shall be by jury; and such trial shall be held in the state where the said crimes shall have been committed; but when not committed within any state, the trial shall be at such place or places as the Congress may by law have directed.

SECTION III. Treason.

Clause 1. Treason against the United States shall consist only in levying war against them, or in adhering to their enemies, giving them aid and comfort. No person shall be convicted of treason unless on the testimony of two witnesses to the same overt act, or on confession in open court.

Clause 2. The Congress shall have power to declare the punishment of treason; but no attainder of treason shall work corruption of blood, or forfeiture, except during the life of the person attainted.

ARTICLE IV.

SECTION I. State Records.

Full faith and credit shall be given in each state to the public acts, records, and judicial proceedings of every other state. And the Congress may, by general laws, prescribe the manner in which such acts, records, and proceedings shall be proved, and the effect thereof.

SECTION II. Privileges of Citizens, etc.

Clause 1. The citizens of each state shall be entitled to all privileges and immunities of citizens in the several states.

Clause 2. A person charged in any state with treason, felony, or other crime, who shall flee from justice and be found in another state, shall, on demand of the executive authority of the state from which he fled, be delivered up, to be removed to the state having jurisdiction of the crime.

Clause 3. No person held to service or labor in one state, under the laws thereof, escaping into another, shall, in consequence of any law or regulation therein, be discharged from such service or labor, but shall be delivered up on claim of the party to whom such service or labor may be due.

SECTION III. New States and Territories.

Clause 1. New states may be admitted by the Congress into this Union, but no new state shall be formed or erected within the jurisdiction of any other state: nor any state be formed by the junction of two or more states, or parts of states, without the consent of the Legislatures of the states concerned, as well as of the Congress.

Clause 2. The Congress shall have power to dispose of, and make all needful rules and regulations respecting the territory or other properly belonging to the United States; and nothing in this Constitution shall be so construed as to prejudice any claims of the United States or of any particular state.

SECTION IV. Guarantee to the States.

The United States shall guarantee to every state in this Union a republican form of government, and shall protect each of them against invasion; and, on application of the Legislature, or of the executive (when the Legislature can not be convened), against domestic violence.

ARTICLE V. POWER OF AMENDMENT.

The Congress, whenever two-thirds of both houses shall deem it necessary, shall propose amendments to this Constitution, or, on the application of the Legislatures of two-thirds of the several states, shall call a convention for proposing amendments, which, in either case, shall be valid to all intents and purposes, as part of this Constitution, when ratified by the Legislatures of three-fourths of the several states, or by conventions in three-fourths thereof, as the one or the other mode of ratification may be proposed by the Congress; provided, that no amendment which may be made prior to the year one thousand eight hundred and eight shall in any manner affect the first and fourth clauses in the ninth section of the first Article; and that no state, without its consent, shall be deprived of its equal suffrage in the Senate.

ARTICLE VI. PUBLIC DEBT, SUPREMACY OF THE CONSTITUTION, OATH OF OFFICE, RELIGIOUS TEST.

Clause 1. All debts contracted and engagements entered into before the adoption of this Constitution, shall be as valid against the United States under this Constitution as under the Confederation.

Clause 2. This Constitution, and the laws of the United States which shall be made in pursuance thereof, and all treaties made, or which shall be made, under the authority of the United States, shall be the supreme law of the land; and the judges in every state shall be bound thereby, any thing in the Constitution or laws of any state to the contrary notwithstanding.

Clause 3. The senators and representatives before mentioned, and the members of the several state Legislatures, and all executive and judicial officers, both of the United States and of the several states, shall be bound by oath or affirmation to support this Constitution; but no religious test shall ever be required as a qualification to any office or public trust under the United States.

## ARTICLE VII. RATIFICATION OF THE CONSTITUTION.

The ratification of the Conventions of nine states shall be sufficient for the establishment of this Constitution between the states so ratifying the same.

Done in Convention, by the unanimous consent of the states present, the seventeenth day of September, in the year of our Lord one thousand seven hundred and eighty-seven, and of the Independence of the United States of America the twelfth. In witness whereof, we have hereunto subscribed our names.

GEORGE WASHINGTON, President and Deputy from Virginia.

New Hampshire.--John Langdon, Nicholas Gilman.

Massachusetts.--Nathaniel Gorham, Rufus King.

Connecticut.--Wm. Samuel Johnson, Roger Sherman.

New York.--Alexander Hamilton.

New Jersey.--William Livingston, William Patterson, David Brearley, Jonathan Dayton.

Pennsylvania,--Benjamin Franklin, Robert Morris, Thomas Fitzsimons, James Wilson, Thomas Mifflin, George Clymer, Jared Ingersoll, Gouverneur Morris.

Delaware.--George Read, John Dickinson, Jacob Broom, Gunning Bedford, Jr., Richard Bassett.

Maryland.--James M'Henry, Daniel Carroll, Daniel of St. Tho. Jenifer.

Virginia.--John Blair, James Madison, Jr.

North Carolina.--William Blount, Hugh Williamson, Richard Dobbs Spaight.

South Carolina.--John Rutledge, Charles Cotesworth Pinckney, Pierce Butler.

Georgia.--William Few, Abraham Baldwin.

Attest, WILLIAM JACKSON, Secretary.

AMENDMENTS TO THE CONSTITUTION.

ARTICLES I--X. Bill of Rights.

ARTICLE I. Congress shall make no law respecting an establishment of religion, or prohibiting the free exercise thereof; or abridging the freedom of speech, or of the press; or the right of the people peaceably to assemble, and to petition the government for a redress of grievances.

ARTICLE II. A well-regulated militia being necessary to the security of a free state, the right of the people to keep and bear arms shall not be infringed.

ARTICLE III. No soldier shall, in time of peace, be quartered in any house without the consent of the owner, nor in time of war, but in a manner to be prescribed by law.

ARTICLE IV. The right of the people to be secure in their persons, houses, papers, and effects, against unreasonable searches and seizures, shall not be violated; and no warrants shall issue but upon probable cause, supported by oath or affirmation, and particularly describing the place to be searched, and the persons or things to be seized.

ARTICLE V. No person shall be held to answer for a capital or otherwise infamous crime, unless on a presentment or indictment of a grand jury, except in cases arising in the land or naval forces, or in the militia when in actual service in time of war or public danger; nor shall any person be subject for the same offense to be twice put in jeopardy of life or limb; nor shall be compelled, in any criminal case, to be a witness against himself; nor be deprived of life, liberty, or property, without due process of law; nor shall private property be taken for public use without just compensation.

ARTICLE VI. In all criminal prosecutions, the accused shall enjoy the right to a speedy and public trial, by an impartial jury of the state and district wherein the crime shall have been committed, which district shall have been previously ascertained by law, and to be informed of the nature and cause of the accusation; to be confronted with the witnesses against him; to have compulsory process for obtaining witnesses in his favor; and to have the assistance of counsel for his defense.

ARTICLE VII. In suits at common law, where the value in controversy shall exceed twenty dollars, the right of trial by jury shall be preserved; and no fact tried by a jury shall be otherwise re-examined in any court of the United States than according to the rules of the common law.

ARTICLE VIII. Excessive bail shall not be required, nor excessive, fines imposed, nor cruel and unusual punishments inflicted.

ARTICLE IX. The enumeration in the Constitution of certain rights shall not be construed to deny or disparage others retained by the people.

ARTICLE X. The powers not delegated to the United States by the Constitution, nor prohibited by it to the states, are reserved to the states respectively or to the people.

ARTICLE XI.

The judicial power of the United States shall not be construed to extend to any suit in law or equity commenced or prosecuted against one of the United States by citizens of another state, or by citizens or subjects of any foreign state.

ARTICLE XII. Mode of choosing the President and Vice-president.

Clause 1. The electors shall meet in their respective states, and vote by ballot for President and Vice-president, one of whom, at least, shall not be an inhabitant of the same state with themselves; they shall name in their ballots the person voted for as President, and in distinct ballots the person voted for as Vice-president; and they shall make distinct lists of all persons voted for as President, and of all persons voted for as Vice-president, and of the number of votes for each, which list they shall sign and certify, and transmit, sealed, to the seat of the government of the United States, directed to the President of the Senate; the President of the Senate shall, in the presence of the Senate and House of Representatives, open all the certificates, and the votes shall then be counted; the person having the greatest number of votes for President shall be the President, if such number be a majority of the whole number of electors appointed; and if no person have such majority, then from the persons having the highest numbers, not exceeding three, on the list of those voted for as President, the House of Representatives shall choose immediately by ballot the President. But in choosing the President, the votes shall be taken by states, the representation from each state having one vote; a quorum for this purpose shall consist of a member or members from two-thirds of the states, and a majority of all the states shall be necessary to a choice. And if the House of Representatives shall not choose a President, whenever the right of choice shall devolve upon them, before the fourth day of March next following, then the Vice-president shall act as President, as in the case of the death or other constitutional disability of the President.

Clause 2. The person having the greatest number of votes as Vice-president shall be the Vice-president, if such number be a majority of the whole number of electors appointed, and if no person have a majority, then from the two highest numbers on the list the Senate shall choose the Vice-president; a quorum for the purpose shall consist of two-thirds of the whole number of senators, and a majority of the whole number shall be necessary to a choice.

Clause 3. But no person constitutionally ineligible to the office of President shall be eligible to that of Vice-president of the United States.

ARTICLE XIII.

SECTION I. Neither slavery nor involuntary servitude, except as a punishment for crime whereof the party shall have been duly convicted, shall exist within the United States, or any place subject to their jurisdiction.

SECTION 2. Congress shall have power to enforce this article by appropriate legislation.

ARTICLE XIV.

SECTION 1. All persons born or naturalized in the United States, and subject to the jurisdiction thereof, are citizens of the United States and of the state wherein they reside. No state shall make or enforce any law which shall abridge the privileges or immunities of citizens of the United States; nor shall any state deprive any person of life, liberty, or property, without due process of law, nor deny to any person within its jurisdiction the equal protection of the laws.

SECTION 2. Representatives shall be apportioned among the several states according to their respective numbers, counting the whole number of persons in each state, excluding Indians not taxed. But when the right to vote at any election for the choice of electors for President and Vice-president of the United States, representatives in Congress, the executive and judicial officers of a state, or the members of the Legislature thereof, is denied to any of the male inhabitants of such state, being twenty-one years of age, and citizens of the United States, or in any way abridged, except for participation in rebellion or other crime, the basis of representation therein shall be reduced in the proportion which the number of such male citizens shall bear to the whole number of male citizens twenty-one years of age in such state.

SECTION 3. No person shall be a senator or representative in Congress, or elector of President and Vice-president, or hold any office, civil or military, under the United States, or under any state, who, having previously taken an oath, as a member of Congress, or as an Officer of the United States, or as a member of any State Legislature, or as an executive or judicial officer of any state, to support the Constitution of the United States, shall have engaged in insurrection or rebellion against the same, or given aid or comfort to the enemies thereof. But Congress may, by a vote of two-thirds of each house, remove such disability.

SECTION 4. The validity of the public debt of the United States, authorized by law, including debts incurred for payment of pensions and bounties for services in suppressing insurrection or rebellion, shall not be questioned. But neither the United States nor any state shall assume or pay any debt or obligation incurred in aid of insurrection or rebellion against the United States, or any claim for the loss or emancipation of any slave; but all such debts, obligations, and claims shall he held illegal and void.

SECTION 5. The Congress shall have power to enforce by appropriate legislation the provisions of this article.

ARTICLE XV.

SECTION 1. The right of citizens of the United States to vote shall not be denied or abridged by the United States or by any state on account of race, color, or previous condition of servitude.

SECTION 2. The Congress shall have power to enforce this article by appropriate legislation.

ARTICLE XVI.

The Congress shall have power to lay and collect taxes on incomes from whatever source derived, without apportionment among the several states, and without regard to any census or enumeration.

ARTICLE XVII.

The Senate of the United States shall be composed of two senators from each state, elected by the people thereof, for six years; and each senator shall have one vote. The electors in each state shall have the qualifications requisite for electors of the most numerous branch of the state legislatures.

When vacancies happen in the representation of any state in the Senate, the executive authority of such state shall issue writs of election to fill such vacancies: Provided, That the legislature of any state may empower the executive thereof to make temporary appointments until the people fill the vacancies by election as the legislature may direct.

This amendment shall not be so construed as to affect the election or term of any senator chosen before it becomes valid as part of the Constitution.

[1]Altered by the 17th Amendment.

[2]Altered by the 12th Amendment.

[3]Altered by the 11th Amendment.

www.ingramcontent.com/pod-product-compliance
Lightning Source LLC
Chambersburg PA
CBHW062006280526
45787CB00005B/1990